ANDROID STUDIO MASTERCLASS

ANDROID IDE FOR APP DEVELOPERS

4 BOOKS IN 1

BOOK 1

ANDROID STUDIO ESSENTIALS: A BEGINNER'S GUIDE TO APP DEVELOPMENT

BOOK 2

ADVANCED ANDROID DEVELOPMENT TECHNIQUES: MASTERING ANDROID STUDIO

BOOK 3

OPTIMIZING PERFORMANCE IN ANDROID STUDIO: EXPERT STRATEGIES FOR EFFICIENT APP DEVELOPMENT

BOOK 4

ANDROID STUDIO PRO: ADVANCED TOOLS AND TIPS FOR POWER USERS

ROB BOTWRIGHT

Published by Rob Botwright
Library of Congress Cataloging-in-Publication Data
ISBN 978-1-83938-758-6
Cover design by Rizzo

Disclaimer

The contents of this book are based on extensive research and the best available historical sources. However, the author and publisher make no claims, promises, or guarantees about the accuracy, completeness, or adequacy of the information contained herein. The information in this book is provided on an "as is" basis, and the author and publisher disclaim any and all liability for any errors, omissions, or inaccuracies in the information or for any actions taken in reliance on such information. The opinions and views expressed in this book are those of the author and do not necessarily reflect the official policy or position of any organization or individual mentioned in this book. Any reference to specific people, places, or events is intended only to provide historical context and is not intended to defame or malign any group, individual, or entity. The information in this book is intended for educational and entertainment purposes only. It is not intended to be a substitute for professional advice or judgment. Readers are encouraged to conduct their own research and to seek professional advice where appropriate. Every effort has been made to obtain necessary permissions and acknowledgments for all images and other copyrighted material used in this book. Any errors or omissions in this regard are unintentional, and the author and publisher will correct them in future editions.

BOOK 1 - ANDROID STUDIO ESSENTIALS: A BEGINNER'S GUIDE TO APP DEVELOPMENT

BOOK - ADVANCED ANDROID DEVELOPMENT TECHNIQUES: MASTERING ANDROID STUDIO

BOOK 3 - OPTIMIZING PERFORMANCE IN ANDROID STUDIO: EXPERT STRATEGIES FOR EFFICIENT APP DEVELOPMENT

BOOK 4 - ANDROID STUDIO PRO: ADVANCED TOOLS AND TIPS FOR POWER USERS

Introduction

Welcome to the "Android Studio Masterclass: Android IDE for App Developers" book bundle, a comprehensive collection designed to equip developers of all levels with the knowledge and skills needed to excel in Android app development. Whether you are just starting your journey or seeking to enhance your expertise, this bundle offers a diverse range of resources to support your growth and success in the dynamic world of Android development.

Within this bundle, you will find four distinct books, each focusing on different aspects of Android Studio and app development. In "Android Studio Essentials: A Beginner's Guide to App Development," beginners will be introduced to the fundamentals of Android development, guiding them through the process of creating their first applications and gaining a solid understanding of the Android Studio environment.

For those looking to advance their skills further, "Advanced Android Development Techniques: Mastering Android Studio" provides an in-depth exploration of advanced features and techniques within Android Studio, empowering developers to tackle complex challenges and build sophisticated applications with confidence.

Performance optimization is a crucial aspect of app development, and "Optimizing Performance in Android Studio: Expert Strategies for Efficient App Development" offers expert insights and strategies for maximizing the performance and efficiency of Android applications, ensuring they deliver a seamless user experience across various devices and scenarios.

Lastly, "Android Studio Pro: Advanced Tools and Tips for Power Users" delves into the realm of advanced tools and customization options within Android Studio, catering to power users seeking to streamline their workflow and unlock the full potential of the IDE.

With a combination of practical guidance, expert insights, and hands-on exercises, this book bundle aims to provide a comprehensive and immersive learning experience for aspiring and seasoned Android developers alike. Whether you are a beginner taking your first steps into Android development or a seasoned professional looking to expand your skill set, the "Android Studio Masterclass" bundle has something to offer for everyone. Let's embark on this journey together and unlock the endless possibilities of Android app development with Android Studio.

BOOK 1

ANDROID STUDIO ESSENTIALS

A BEGINNER'S GUIDE TO APP DEVELOPMENT

ROB BOTWRIGHT

Chapter 1: Understanding the Android Studio Interface

Interface layout overview is crucial for developers as it forms the foundation of any user interface (UI) design. The interface layout refers to the arrangement and organization of elements within a graphical user interface (GUI) or a command-line interface (CLI). In GUIs, this includes the positioning of buttons, text fields, images, and other UI components, while in CLIs, it involves the structure of commands and their parameters. Understanding interface layout is essential for creating intuitive and user-friendly applications that provide a seamless experience for users.

In GUI-based applications, the interface layout plays a significant role in determining the overall user experience. A well-designed layout can enhance usability, improve navigation, and facilitate task completion. Conversely, a poorly designed layout can confuse users, hinder productivity, and lead to frustration. Therefore, developers need to pay careful attention to the layout of their applications to ensure optimal usability and user satisfaction.

One important aspect of interface layout is the concept of visual hierarchy. Visual hierarchy refers to the arrangement of elements on the screen in a way that guides the user's attention and helps them understand the relative importance of each element. Elements that are more important or frequently used should be given greater prominence, while less important elements should be de-emphasized. This can be achieved through the use of size, color, contrast, and spacing.

Another consideration in interface layout is consistency. Consistency ensures that similar elements are presented in a uniform manner throughout the application, making it easier for users to understand and navigate. Consistent layout patterns help users develop mental models of how the application works, reducing cognitive load and improving usability.

In GUI-based applications, developers often use layout managers to arrange UI components within containers such as windows, panels, or frames. Layout managers automatically adjust the position and size of components based on factors such as screen size, orientation, and user preferences. Common layout managers include BorderLayout, FlowLayout, GridLayout, and GridBagLayout in Java Swing applications.

In web development, Cascading Style Sheets (CSS) are used to control the layout and appearance of web pages. CSS provides a powerful set of tools for defining the positioning, size, and styling of HTML elements, allowing developers to create responsive and visually appealing interfaces across different devices and screen sizes. Techniques such as Flexbox and CSS Grid Layout offer flexible and efficient ways to create complex layouts with minimal code.

In CLI-based applications, interface layout is primarily concerned with the organization and presentation of commands and their options. Developers must design intuitive command structures that are easy to understand and use, even for users with little or no technical expertise. This often involves grouping related commands together, providing clear descriptions and usage examples, and offering built-in help and documentation.

Deploying the techniques discussed above requires a combination of design principles, development tools, and best practices. Developers can use prototyping tools such as Adobe XD, Sketch, or Figma to create mockups and wireframes of their interface layouts before writing any code. These tools allow for rapid iteration and experimentation, enabling developers to refine their designs based on user feedback and usability testing.

Once the interface layout has been finalized, developers can use programming languages and frameworks such as Java, Kotlin, Swift, React, or Angular to implement the design in code. GUI-based applications typically use event-driven programming models, where user actions such as clicks, taps, and keystrokes trigger corresponding responses from the application. Developers must write event handlers and callback functions to respond to these events and update the interface accordingly.

In web development, developers use HTML, CSS, and JavaScript to create interactive and dynamic user interfaces. HTML provides the structure and content of web pages, CSS controls the layout and styling, and JavaScript adds interactivity and behavior. Modern web development frameworks such as React, Angular, and Vue.js offer powerful tools and libraries for building complex and responsive web interfaces with minimal effort.

In CLI-based applications, developers typically use programming languages such as Python, Ruby, or Bash to implement the command-line interface and associated functionality. Command-line applications often rely on libraries and frameworks such as argparse in Python or OptionParser in Ruby to parse command-line arguments and options, validate input, and provide help and usage information.

Overall, interface layout is a critical aspect of application design and development that requires careful consideration and planning. By following best practices and leveraging appropriate tools and techniques, developers can create interfaces that are intuitive, efficient, and visually appealing, leading to a positive user experience and improved user satisfaction.

Navigating tool windows is a fundamental skill for developers working with integrated development environments (IDEs) like Android Studio, Visual Studio Code, or IntelliJ IDEA. These tool windows provide access to various features and functionalities essential for software development, including project navigation, code editing, debugging, version control, and more. Mastering the navigation of tool windows can significantly improve productivity and efficiency in the development workflow.

In Android Studio, one of the most widely used IDEs for Android app development, navigating tool windows is an integral part of the development process. Android Studio offers a plethora of tool windows, each serving a specific purpose and providing access to different aspects of the project. The most commonly used tool windows in Android Studio include the Project window, the Editor window, the Navigation window, the Terminal window, and the Logcat window, among others.

To navigate between tool windows in Android Studio, developers can use keyboard shortcuts or the mouse. The default keymap for Android Studio includes shortcuts for quickly switching between different tool windows. For example, pressing Alt + 1 on Windows or Command + 1 on macOS focuses the Project window, while Alt + 7 or Command + 7 focuses the Structure window, which displays the structure of the currently edited file.

Alternatively, developers can use the mouse to navigate between tool windows by clicking on the corresponding tabs located on the left and right sides of the IDE window. Android Studio allows users to customize the layout of tool windows by dragging and rearranging tabs to suit their preferences. This flexibility enables developers to create a workspace that maximizes efficiency and minimizes distractions.

In addition to navigating between predefined tool windows, Android Studio also allows developers to create custom tool windows tailored to their specific needs. Custom tool windows can display project-specific information, provide quick access to frequently used actions, or integrate third-party plugins and extensions. Creating a custom tool window in Android Studio typically involves writing a plugin using the IntelliJ Platform Plugin SDK and registering the tool window with the IDE.

Visual Studio Code (VS Code), another popular IDE used for web development, also offers a wide range of tool windows to support various workflows. In VS Code, tool windows are referred to as "views" and include the Explorer view, the Source Control view, the Debug view, the Extensions view, and many others. Navigating between views in VS Code is similar to navigating between tool windows in Android Studio, with keyboard shortcuts and mouse clicks being the primary methods of interaction.

To navigate between views in VS Code using keyboard shortcuts, developers can press Ctrl + Shift + E to focus the Explorer view, Ctrl + Shift + D to focus the Debug view, and Ctrl + Shift + X to focus the Extensions view, among others. Alternatively, developers can use the mouse to click on the icons located on the activity bar on the side of the VS Code window to switch between views quickly.

In addition to built-in views, VS Code also supports the creation of custom views through extensions. Extensions in VS Code can contribute custom views to the IDE, allowing developers to extend the functionality of the editor and tailor it to their specific needs. Creating a custom view in VS Code involves writing an extension using the VS Code Extension API and registering the view with the editor.

In the context of command-line interfaces (CLIs), navigating tool windows translates to navigating between different terminal windows or tabs. CLIs are commonly used by developers for tasks such as running commands, managing files, and interacting with version control systems. Most modern operating systems provide built-in support for multiple terminal windows or tabs, allowing developers to work with multiple command-line sessions simultaneously.

In Unix-based operating systems like Linux and macOS, developers can use terminal multiplexers such as tmux or GNU Screen to manage multiple terminal sessions within a single window. These tools allow developers to create, detach, and reattach terminal sessions, switch between sessions, and split the terminal window into multiple panes for multitasking. Terminal multiplexers are especially useful for remote development scenarios where access to a graphical IDE may be limited.

In Windows, developers can use the built-in Command Prompt or Windows PowerShell to work with the command-line interface. Windows also supports third-party terminal emulators such as ConEmu or Windows Terminal, which provide advanced features like tabs, panes, and customizable keyboard shortcuts. Navigating between terminal windows or tabs in Windows typically involves using keyboard shortcuts or clicking on the corresponding icons in the terminal emulator's user interface.

In summary, navigating tool windows is an essential skill for developers working with IDEs and CLIs. Whether developing mobile apps, web applications, or command-line utilities, understanding how to efficiently navigate between different tool windows or terminal sessions can greatly enhance productivity and streamline the development process. By mastering keyboard shortcuts, mouse interactions, and customizations, developers can create a personalized workspace that maximizes efficiency and minimizes distractions.

Chapter 2: Setting Up Your First Android Project

Creating project structure is a foundational step in software development, essential for organizing code, resources, and dependencies in a systematic manner. A well-structured project layout promotes maintainability, scalability, and collaboration among team members throughout the development lifecycle. Whether working on a small script or a large-scale application, establishing a clear and consistent project structure is crucial for efficient development and future maintenance.

In modern software development, project structure often follows established conventions and best practices specific to the programming language or framework being used. For example, in Java projects, it's common to organize source code files into packages based on their functionality or domain, while in web development, projects are typically structured around the Model-View-Controller (MVC) pattern or similar architectural paradigms.

One widely used approach for organizing project structure is the concept of directory hierarchies. A directory hierarchy consists of nested directories and subdirectories, each serving a specific purpose within the project. By dividing code and resources into logical units, developers can easily locate files, manage dependencies, and enforce separation of concerns.

In many programming languages and frameworks, there are established conventions for organizing project structure. For example, in Java projects using the Maven build system, source code files are typically located in the src/main/java directory, while resources such as configuration files and static assets are placed in src/main/resources. Similarly, test code is conventionally stored in src/test/java and test resources in src/test/resources.

In web development, project structure often revolves around the separation of concerns principle, which advocates for dividing code into distinct layers responsible for different aspects of the application. For example, in a typical web application following the MVC pattern, the project structure may include directories for models, views, and controllers, as well as additional directories for static assets, templates, and configuration files.

Creating a well-structured project layout begins with understanding the requirements and architecture of the application. Developers should carefully consider factors such as the size and complexity of the project, the technologies and frameworks being used, and the anticipated future growth and maintenance requirements. By planning ahead and establishing clear guidelines for project structure, developers can avoid confusion and inconsistencies down the line.

Once the project requirements are clear, developers can begin creating the initial directory structure. This typically involves creating directories for source code, resources, tests, documentation, and build artifacts. In addition, developers may create directories for specific modules, components, or features of the application, depending on its architecture and design.

In many cases, project structure is managed and enforced by build tools and project scaffolding utilities. For example, build tools like Maven, Gradle, and npm provide project templates and conventions for organizing code and resources. These tools often generate a default project structure based on the chosen template, allowing developers to focus on writing code rather than configuring directory layouts.

In Java projects using Maven or Gradle, developers can use the respective build tool's project initialization commands to create a new project with a predefined structure. For example, to create a new Maven project, developers can use the mvn archetype:generate command, which prompts them to select a project template from a list of available options. Similarly, in Gradle projects, developers can use the gradle init command to generate a new project with a default directory structure.

In web development, project structure often varies depending on the chosen framework or library. For example, in a React.js project created with Create React App, the project structure includes directories for source code, tests, and configuration files, as well as a public directory for static assets. Similarly, in a Django project, the project structure follows the conventions of the Django framework, with directories for models, views, templates, and static files.

In addition to organizing code and resources, project structure often includes configuration files and build scripts necessary for building, testing, and deploying the application. These files typically reside in the project root directory and provide instructions for tools and services used in the development process. Common configuration files include package.json in Node.js projects, pom.xml in Maven projects, and build.gradle in Gradle projects.

Maintaining project structure is an ongoing process that requires attention to detail and adherence to established conventions. As the project evolves and new features are added, developers may need to refactor the project structure to accommodate changes and ensure maintainability. This may involve reorganizing directories, splitting or merging modules, or updating build scripts to reflect the updated layout.

In summary, creating a well-structured project layout is essential for successful software development. By organizing code, resources, and dependencies in a systematic manner, developers can improve maintainability, scalability, and collaboration throughout the development lifecycle. By following established conventions and best practices, developers can create projects that are easy to navigate, understand, and extend, leading to more efficient development and higher-quality software.

Setting dependencies is a critical aspect of software development, ensuring that projects have access to the necessary libraries, frameworks, and packages to function properly. Dependencies are external resources that a project relies on to compile, build, and run successfully, and managing them effectively is essential for maintaining project stability and consistency. In modern software development, dependency management tools and techniques play a crucial role in simplifying the process of setting up and managing dependencies across different projects and environments.

One of the most common approaches to setting dependencies is through the use of package managers, which are specialized tools designed to automate the process of downloading, installing, and managing dependencies. Package managers provide a centralized repository of software packages, making it easy for developers to search for and install the dependencies they need for their projects. Different programming languages and platforms have their own package managers, each with its own set of commands and conventions for setting dependencies.

In JavaScript development, npm (Node Package Manager) is the de facto package manager for Node.js and front-end

JavaScript projects. To set dependencies using npm, developers typically create a package.json file in the root directory of their project and use the npm install command to install dependencies listed in the package.json file. For example, to install the lodash library as a dependency for a Node.js project, developers can run the following command:

bashCopy code

```
npm install lodash
```

This command will download the lodash package from the npm registry and add it to the project's node_modules directory, as well as update the dependencies section of the package.json file with the latest version of lodash.

Similarly, in Python development, pip is the standard package manager for installing Python packages from the Python Package Index (PyPI). To set dependencies using pip, developers typically create a requirements.txt file listing the required packages and use the pip install command to install them. For example, to install the requests library as a dependency for a Python project, developers can create a requirements.txt file with the following content:

plaintextCopy code

```
requests==2.26.0
```

Then, they can use the following command to install the dependencies listed in the requirements.txt file:

bashCopy code

```
pip install -r requirements.txt
```

This command will download and install the requests library, along with any other dependencies listed in the requirements.txt file, into the project's virtual environment.

In Java development, Maven and Gradle are two popular build automation tools that also serve as package managers for managing Java dependencies. In Maven, developers specify dependencies in the project's pom.xml (Project

Object Model) file, while in Gradle, dependencies are declared in the build.gradle file. Both Maven and Gradle automatically download and manage dependencies from central repositories such as Maven Central. For example, to add the JUnit testing framework as a dependency in a Maven project, developers can add the following dependency declaration to the pom.xml file:

xmlCopy code

```
<dependency> <groupId>junit</groupId> <artifactId>junit</artifactId> <version>4.13.2</version> <scope>test</scope> </dependency>
```

Similarly, in Gradle, developers can add the following dependency declaration to the build.gradle file:

groovyCopy code

```
testImplementation 'junit:junit:4.13.2'
```

Both Maven and Gradle provide commands for fetching and installing dependencies, such as mvn install and ./gradlew dependencies, respectively.

In addition to package managers, version control systems such as Git also play a role in dependency management, particularly in projects with multiple contributors or dependencies hosted on version control platforms. By specifying dependencies in a project's version control repository, developers can ensure that all contributors have access to the same set of dependencies and can easily reproduce the project's environment. Git submodules and Git subtree are two Git features that allow developers to include external repositories as dependencies in their projects. Using submodules or subtrees, developers can add a reference to an external Git repository as a subdirectory within their project, making it easy to track changes and updates to the dependency over time.

Another common approach to setting dependencies is through the use of dependency injection frameworks, which automate the process of wiring together different components and services within an application. Dependency injection frameworks such as Spring Framework for Java and Angular for TypeScript/JavaScript provide mechanisms for declaring dependencies and managing their lifecycles, reducing the complexity of manual dependency management. In Spring Framework, for example, developers can use annotations such as @Autowired and @Inject to inject dependencies into components at runtime, while in Angular, developers can use the constructor to declare dependencies and let Angular's dependency injection system resolve them automatically.

In addition to managing runtime dependencies, developers also need to consider build-time dependencies, which are dependencies required for compiling, testing, and building the project but are not needed at runtime. Build tools such as Maven, Gradle, and npm provide mechanisms for specifying build-time dependencies separately from runtime dependencies, allowing developers to optimize the size and performance of their applications by excluding unnecessary dependencies from production builds.

Overall, setting dependencies is a fundamental aspect of software development that requires careful consideration and planning. By leveraging package managers, version control systems, dependency injection frameworks, and build tools, developers can streamline the process of managing dependencies and ensure that their projects have access to the resources they need to succeed. With the right tools and techniques in place, developers can focus on writing code and building innovative solutions without being bogged down by dependency management issues.

Chapter 3: Exploring Basic UI Components

Understanding views is fundamental in software development, particularly in user interface (UI) design and development. Views are the building blocks of graphical user interfaces (GUIs), representing visual elements such as buttons, text fields, images, and containers that users interact with when using an application. Having a deep understanding of views is essential for creating intuitive, responsive, and visually appealing user interfaces that meet the needs and expectations of users across different platforms and devices.

In the context of Android app development, views are represented by subclasses of the View class or its subclasses, such as Button, TextView, ImageView, and ViewGroup. Each view is responsible for rendering a specific UI element on the screen and responding to user interactions, such as clicks, swipes, and touches. Views can be arranged and nested within layouts to create complex UI designs, with each view contributing to the overall user experience.

To understand views in Android development, it's important to grasp the concept of the view hierarchy, which defines the structure and relationships between views in an Android application. The view hierarchy is typically represented as a tree, with the root view at the top and child views nested underneath. Views are arranged hierarchically based on their containment relationships, with parent views containing and managing the layout and positioning of their child views.

In Android Studio, developers can use the Layout Editor to visually design and manipulate views within layouts. The Layout Editor provides a graphical interface for dragging and dropping views onto the canvas, resizing and positioning views, and configuring their properties. By using the Layout Editor, developers can create and modify UI layouts with ease, without having to write XML code manually.

In addition to the Layout Editor, developers can also define views and layouts using XML markup in Android resource files. XML layouts provide a declarative way to specify the structure, properties, and behavior of views in an Android application. By defining views and layouts in XML, developers can separate the presentation layer from the business logic, making it easier to maintain and update the UI over time.

For example, the following XML code defines a simple layout with a TextView and a Button arranged vertically:

xmlCopy code

```
<LinearLayout
xmlns:android="http://schemas.android.com/apk/res/andro
id" android:layout_width="match_parent"
android:layout_height="match_parent"
android:orientation="vertical"> <TextView
android:id="@+id/text_view"
android:layout_width="wrap_content"
android:layout_height="wrap_content" android:text="Hello,
World!" /> <Button android:id="@+id/button"
android:layout_width="wrap_content"
android:layout_height="wrap_content" android:text="Click
Me" /> </LinearLayout>
```

This layout consists of a LinearLayout as the root view, with a TextView and a Button as its child views. The orientation attribute of the LinearLayout specifies that its child views should be arranged vertically.

Understanding views also involves knowing how to customize their appearance and behavior to align with the design and functionality requirements of the application.

Views in Android can be customized using various attributes and properties defined in XML or programmatically in Java or Kotlin code. For example, developers can change the text color, font size, and background color of a TextView by modifying its attributes in XML or calling setter methods in code.

In addition to basic customization, views in Android can also be styled using themes and styles to achieve a consistent look and feel across the application. Themes define the overall visual style of an application, including colors, fonts, and layout parameters, while styles allow developers to define reusable sets of attributes that can be applied to individual views or entire layouts.

To apply a theme to an Android application, developers can specify the theme in the AndroidManifest.xml file using the android:theme attribute of the application element. Themes can be defined in XML resource files or programmatically in code, allowing developers to create custom themes tailored to their specific design requirements.

xmlCopy code

```
<application android:theme="@style/AppTheme"> ... </application>
```

Understanding views also involves knowing how to handle user interactions and events generated by views in an Android application. Views in Android can respond to various types of user input, such as clicks, touches, swipes, and gestures, by implementing event listeners and callback methods.

For example, to handle a click event on a Button view, developers can set an OnClickListener on the Button object and override the onClick method to define the behavior that should occur when the button is clicked. This can be done programmatically in Java or Kotlin code or declaratively in XML using the android:onClick attribute.

javaCopy code

```
Button button = findViewById(R.id.button); button.setOnClickListener(new View.OnClickListener() { @Override public void onClick(View v) { // Handle button click event } });
```

Alternatively, developers can define an onClick attribute in the XML layout file and specify the name of the method to be called when the button is clicked.

xmlCopy code

```
<Button android:id="@+id/button" android:layout_width="wrap_content" android:layout_height="wrap_content" android:text="Click Me" android:onClick="onButtonClick" />
```

javaCopy code

```
public void onButtonClick(View view) { // Handle button click event }
```

Understanding views is essential for creating engaging and user-friendly applications across various platforms and devices. By mastering the concepts and techniques related to views, developers can design and develop UIs that meet the needs and expectations of users, leading to a positive user experience and increased user satisfaction. With the right knowledge and skills, developers can leverage views to create visually stunning and highly functional applications that stand out in today's competitive app market.

Working with ViewGroups is essential in user interface (UI) design and development, especially in Android app development, where ViewGroups play a crucial role in organizing and managing the layout of UI elements on the screen. ViewGroups are a subclass of the View class in Android and provide containers for holding and arranging other views, known as child views, in a hierarchical manner.

Understanding how to work with ViewGroups is fundamental for creating complex and responsive UI designs that adapt to different screen sizes and orientations, providing a seamless user experience across various Android devices.

In Android development, ViewGroup is an abstract class that serves as the base class for all layout containers, such as LinearLayout, RelativeLayout, FrameLayout, ConstraintLayout, and others. Each ViewGroup subclass implements its own layout algorithm and rules for positioning and sizing child views within its boundaries. By combining different ViewGroup subclasses and nesting them hierarchically, developers can create intricate UI layouts that meet the design requirements of their applications.

To work with ViewGroups in Android, developers typically use XML layout files to define the structure and properties of ViewGroup containers and their child views. XML layouts provide a declarative way to specify the arrangement and behavior of UI elements, making it easy to visualize and maintain complex UI designs. Developers can use layout attributes such as layout_width, layout_height, layout_margin, layout_gravity, and others to customize the appearance and positioning of ViewGroup containers and their child views.

For example, the following XML code defines a LinearLayout container with two TextView child views arranged vertically:

xmlCopy code

```
<LinearLayout
xmlns:android="http://schemas.android.com/apk/res/andro
id" android:layout_width="match_parent"
android:layout_height="match_parent"
android:orientation="vertical"> <TextView
android:id="@+id/text_view1"
android:layout_width="match_parent"
```

android:layout_height="wrap_content"
android:text="TextView 1" /> <TextView
android:id="@+id/text_view2"
android:layout_width="match_parent"
android:layout_height="wrap_content"
android:text="TextView 2" /> </LinearLayout>

In this layout, the LinearLayout container is configured to arrange its child views vertically, using the android:orientation="vertical" attribute. The layout_width and layout_height attributes of the TextView child views are set to match_parent and wrap_content, respectively, specifying that the views should fill the width of the parent container and wrap their content vertically.

To work with ViewGroup containers programmatically in Android, developers can use the ViewGroup class and its subclasses to create and manipulate layout containers dynamically at runtime. For example, to create a LinearLayout container programmatically and add TextView child views to it, developers can use the following Java code:

javaCopy code

```
LinearLayout linearLayout = new LinearLayout(context);
linearLayout.setLayoutParams( new
LinearLayout.LayoutParams(
LinearLayout.LayoutParams.MATCH_PARENT,
LinearLayout.LayoutParams.MATCH_PARENT ));
linearLayout.setOrientation(LinearLayout.VERTICAL);
TextView textView1 = new TextView(context);
textView1.setText( "TextView 1" );
linearLayout.addView(textView1); TextView textView2 =
new TextView(context); textView2.setText( "TextView 2" );
linearLayout.addView(textView2);
```

In this code snippet, a new LinearLayout container is created using the LinearLayout constructor, and layout parameters are set programmatically using the setLayoutParams method. Child TextView views are created dynamically using the TextView constructor, and their text content is set using the setText method. Finally, the child views are added to the LinearLayout container using the addView method.

Working with ViewGroups also involves understanding layout attributes and properties that affect the positioning and sizing of child views within ViewGroup containers. Android provides a wide range of layout attributes and properties that developers can use to customize the appearance and behavior of UI elements in their applications.

For example, the layout_gravity attribute specifies how a child view should be positioned within its parent ViewGroup container, while the layout_weight attribute specifies the relative weight of a child view within a LinearLayout container. These attributes allow developers to create flexible and responsive UI layouts that adapt to different screen sizes and orientations.

In addition to basic layout attributes, Android also provides more advanced layout managers and constraints that enable developers to create complex UI designs with precise control over the positioning and sizing of UI elements. For example, the ConstraintLayout container allows developers to create responsive UI layouts by defining constraints between child views, such as aligning views to each other or to the parent container's edges.

To work with ConstraintLayout in Android, developers can use the Layout Editor in Android Studio to visually design UI layouts and create constraints between UI elements. The Layout Editor provides a graphical interface for adding and editing views, dragging constraints between views, and previewing layouts on different devices and screen sizes. Developers can also define constraints programmatically in XML layout files using attributes such as app:layout_constraintTop_toTopOf and app:layout_constraintStart_toStartOf.

xmlCopy code

```
<androidx.constraintlayout.widget.ConstraintLayout
xmlns:android="http://schemas.android.com/apk/res/andro
id" xmlns:app="http://schemas.android.com/apk/res-auto"
android:layout_width="match_parent"
android:layout_height="match_parent"> <TextView
android:id="@+id/text_view1"
android:layout_width="wrap_content"
android:layout_height="wrap_content"
android:text="TextView 1"
app:layout_constraintTop_toTopOf="parent"
app:layout_constraintStart_toStartOf="parent"
app:layout_constraintEnd_toEndOf="parent" /> <TextView
android:id="@+id/text_view2"
android:layout_width="wrap_content"
android:layout_height="wrap_content"
android:text="TextView 2"
app:layout_constraintTop_toBottomOf="@id/text_view1"
app:layout_constraintStart_toStartOf="parent"
app:layout_constraintEnd_toEndOf="parent" />
</androidx.constraintlayout.widget.ConstraintLayout>
```

In this layout, TextView 1 is constrained to the top, start, and end edges of the parent ConstraintLayout container, while TextView 2 is constrained below TextView 1 and aligned with the start and end edges of the parent container.

Working with ViewGroups is an essential skill for Android developers, enabling them to create flexible, responsive, and visually appealing UI layouts for their applications. By understanding the concepts and techniques related to ViewGroups, developers can design and implement UIs that meet the needs and expectations of users, providing a seamless and enjoyable user experience on Android devices of all shapes and sizes. With the right knowledge and skills, developers can leverage ViewGroups to create innovative and engaging applications that stand out in the competitive Android app market.

Chapter 4: Handling User Input: Buttons, Text Fields, and More

Button functionality is a crucial aspect of user interface (UI) design and development in various software applications, serving as a primary means for users to interact with and control the application's behavior. Buttons are graphical elements that users can click, tap, or press to trigger specific actions or events within an application, such as submitting a form, navigating to a different screen, or performing a task. Understanding how to implement and customize button functionality is essential for creating intuitive, responsive, and user-friendly applications across different platforms and devices.

In Android app development, buttons are represented by the Button class or its subclasses, such as ImageButton, FloatingActionButton, and others. Buttons can be added to layouts using XML markup or programmatically in Java or Kotlin code, and developers can customize their appearance, behavior, and functionality to align with the design and requirements of the application.

To create a button in an Android layout XML file, developers can use the <Button> element and specify attributes such as android:id, android:text, android:layout_width, and android:layout_height to define the button's appearance and text label. For example:

xmlCopy code

```
<Button android:id="@+id/submit_button"
android:layout_width="wrap_content"
android:layout_height="wrap_content"
android:text="Submit" />
```

This XML code snippet defines a simple button with the text label "Submit" and default layout width and height. The android:id attribute assigns a unique identifier to the button, allowing developers to reference it in code and handle user interactions programmatically.

To handle button clicks and define the actions or events triggered by the button, developers can set an OnClickListener on the button object and override the onClick method to specify the desired behavior. In Java, this can be done as follows:

javaCopy code

```
Button submitButton = findViewById(R.id.submit_button); submitButton.setOnClickListener(new View.OnClickListener() { @Override public void onClick(View v) { // Handle button click event // Perform actions such as form submission, navigation, etc. } });
```

In this code snippet, an OnClickListener is set on the submitButton object, and the onClick method is overridden to define the behavior that should occur when the button is clicked. Inside the onClick method, developers can implement logic to perform actions such as form submission, navigation to another activity or fragment, data processing, or any other task required by the application.

Alternatively, developers can define the onClick attribute directly in the XML layout file and specify the name of the method to be called when the button is clicked. For example:

xmlCopy code

```
<Button android:id="@+id/submit_button" android:layout_width="wrap_content" android:layout_height="wrap_content" android:text="Submit" android:onClick="onSubmitButtonClick" />
```

In this case, the onSubmitButtonClick method must be defined in the activity or fragment associated with the layout XML file, and it will be automatically invoked when the button is clicked.

javaCopy code

```java
public void onSubmitButtonClick(View view) { // Handle button click event // Perform actions such as form submission, navigation, etc. }
```

By using either approach, developers can define the functionality of buttons in Android applications and respond to user interactions effectively.

In addition to handling button clicks, developers can customize the appearance and behavior of buttons in Android applications by applying styles, themes, and attributes. For example, developers can use attributes such as android:background, android:textColor, android:textSize, and others to customize the visual appearance of buttons, such as background color, text color, text size, padding, and margins.

xmlCopy code

```xml
<Button android:id="@+id/submit_button" android:layout_width="wrap_content" android:layout_height="wrap_content" android:text="Submit" android:background="@drawable/custom_button_background" android:textColor="@color/custom_text_color" android:textSize="18sp" android:padding="12dp" android:layout_marginTop="16dp" android:layout_marginBottom="16dp" />
```

In this example, the button's background color, text color, text size, padding, and margins are customized using attributes defined in the XML layout file. Developers can also use drawable resources, color resources, dimension resources, and other XML resources to provide consistent styling across the application and support theming and customization.

In addition to standard buttons, Android also provides specialized button subclasses such as ImageButton and FloatingActionButton, which offer additional functionality and styling options. ImageButton allows developers to use custom images or icons as button backgrounds, while FloatingActionButton provides a floating action button design commonly used for primary actions in applications.

To create an ImageButton in Android, developers can use the <ImageButton> element in XML layout files and specify the android:src attribute to set the image or icon to be displayed on the button.

xmlCopy code

```
<ImageButton android:id="@+id/image_button"
android:layout_width="wrap_content"
android:layout_height="wrap_content"
android:src="@drawable/ic_action_name" />
```

Similarly, FloatingActionButton can be created using the <com.google.android.material.floatingactionbutton.Floating ActionButton> element, which is part of the Material Components library provided by Google.

xmlCopy code

```
<com.google.android.material.floatingactionbutton.Floating
ActionButton android:id="@+id/floating_action_button"
android:layout_width="wrap_content"
android:layout_height="wrap_content"
android:src="@drawable/ic_action_name"
app:backgroundTint="@color/colorPrimary"
app:fabSize="normal" />
```

In this example, the FloatingActionButton is customized using attributes such as app:backgroundTint to set the

button background color and app:fabSize to specify the button size.
Working with buttons is an essential skill for Android developers, enabling them to create interactive and engaging user interfaces for their applications. By understanding how to implement button functionality, customize button appearance, and respond to user interactions, developers can create intuitive and user-friendly applications that meet the needs and expectations of users. With the right knowledge and skills, developers can leverage buttons to enhance the usability, accessibility, and overall user experience of their Android applications, leading to higher user satisfaction and adoption.

Text fields implementation is a fundamental aspect of user interface (UI) design and development, playing a crucial role in capturing user input, displaying information, and enabling communication between users and applications. Text fields are graphical elements that allow users to enter and edit text-based data, such as usernames, passwords, search queries, and messages, making them an essential component of various software applications across different platforms and devices. Understanding how to implement and customize text fields is essential for creating intuitive, responsive, and user-friendly interfaces that meet the needs and expectations of users.
In Android app development, text fields are represented by the EditText class, which is a subclass of the TextView class and provides an editable text field that users can interact with using the keyboard or other input methods. EditText views can be added to layouts using XML markup or programmatically in Java or Kotlin code, and developers can customize their appearance, behavior, and functionality to suit the requirements of their applications.

To create a basic text field in an Android layout XML file, developers can use the <EditText> element and specify attributes such as android:id, android:hint, android:layout_width, and android:layout_height to define the text field's appearance and behavior. For example:

xmlCopy code

```
<EditText android:id="@+id/username_edit_text"
android:layout_width="match_parent"
android:layout_height="wrap_content" android:hint="Enter
your username" />
```

This XML code snippet defines a simple EditText view with a hint text "Enter your username" that provides guidance to the user on what information to input. The android:id attribute assigns a unique identifier to the EditText view, allowing developers to reference it in code and retrieve the entered text.

To retrieve the text entered by the user in an EditText view programmatically, developers can use the getText() method to obtain a CharSequence object representing the text content of the EditText view. For example:

javaCopy code

```
EditText usernameEditText =
findViewById(R.id.username_edit_text); CharSequence
username = usernameEditText.getText();
```

In this code snippet, the getText() method is called on the usernameEditText object to retrieve the text entered by the user in the EditText view. The returned CharSequence object can then be converted to a String or used directly to access and manipulate the text content.

In addition to basic text input, EditText views in Android can be customized and configured to support various input types, such as email addresses, phone numbers, dates, passwords, and multi-line text. Developers can use the android:inputType attribute to specify the desired input type for an EditText view, which affects the behavior of the keyboard and input method editor (IME) when interacting with the text field.

For example, to create an EditText view for entering email addresses, developers can use the following XML code:

xmlCopy code

```
<EditText android:id="@+id/email_edit_text"
android:layout_width="match_parent"
android:layout_height="wrap_content" android:hint="Enter
your email" android:inputType="textEmailAddress" />
```

In this example, the android:inputType attribute is set to "textEmailAddress", indicating that the EditText view should expect input in the form of an email address. As a result, the keyboard and IME will display appropriate suggestions and auto-corrections for email addresses when the user interacts with the text field.

In addition to standard text fields, Android also provides specialized text field subclasses such as TextInputLayout and AutoCompleteTextView, which offer additional features and functionality for text input and validation.

TextInputLayout is a container view that wraps an EditText view and provides support for floating labels, error messages, and input validation. It enhances the usability and accessibility of text fields by displaying the hint text as a floating label above the EditText view when the field is focused or has content, providing visual feedback to users.

To use TextInputLayout in an Android layout XML file, developers can wrap an EditText view with a <com.google.android.material.textfield.TextInputLayout> element and specify attributes such as android:id, app:hint, and app:errorEnabled to customize its behavior and appearance. For example:

xmlCopy code

```xml
<com.google.android.material.textfield.TextInputLayout
android:id="@+id/email_input_layout"
android:layout_width="match_parent"
android:layout_height="wrap_content"    app:hint="Email">
<EditText                   android:id="@+id/email_edit_text"
android:layout_width="match_parent"
android:layout_height="wrap_content"
android:inputType="textEmailAddress"                    />
</com.google.android.material.textfield.TextInputLayout>
```

In this layout, the EditText view is wrapped with a TextInputLayout container, and the hint text "Email" is specified using the app:hint attribute. The android:inputType attribute is also set to "textEmailAddress" to indicate that the EditText view should expect input in the form of an email address.

AutoCompleteTextView is another specialized text field subclass in Android that provides auto-completion suggestions based on user input, enhancing the efficiency and accuracy of text input in applications. AutoCompleteTextView can be used to create text fields that offer predictive suggestions as the user types, reducing the need for manual entry and improving the user experience.

To use AutoCompleteTextView in an Android layout XML file, developers can use the <AutoCompleteTextView> element and specify attributes such as android:id, android:layout_width, android:layout_height, and android:completionThreshold to configure its behavior and appearance. For example:

xmlCopy code

```xml
<AutoCompleteTextView
android:id="@+id/search_auto_complete_text_view"
android:layout_width="match_parent"
```

```
android:layout_height="wrap_content"
android:hint="Search" android:completionThreshold="1" />
```

In this layout, the AutoCompleteTextView is configured with a hint text "Search" and a completion threshold of 1, indicating that auto-completion suggestions should be provided after typing at least one character. Developers can provide a list of suggestions to the AutoCompleteTextView using adapters such as ArrayAdapter or CursorAdapter, allowing users to select from a predefined set of options or dynamically generated suggestions.

Working with text fields is an essential skill for Android developers, enabling them to create interactive and user-friendly interfaces for their applications. By understanding how to implement and customize text fields, developers can create intuitive and efficient text input experiences that meet the needs and expectations of users. With the right knowledge and skills, developers can leverage text fields to enhance the usability, accessibility, and overall user experience of their Android applications, leading to higher user satisfaction and engagement.

Chapter 5: Navigating Between Screens with Activities and Intents

The Activity Lifecycle in Android development is a crucial concept that developers must understand thoroughly to create robust and responsive applications that provide a seamless user experience across various devices and scenarios. Activities are a fundamental building block of Android applications, representing individual screens with which users can interact. Understanding the lifecycle of activities is essential for managing their behavior and state throughout their lifecycle, from creation to destruction, and handling transitions between different states effectively.

In Android, the lifecycle of an activity is governed by a set of callback methods that are invoked by the system at different points in the activity's lifespan. These callback methods allow developers to perform initialization, cleanup, and other tasks in response to changes in the activity's state. By implementing these callback methods correctly, developers can ensure that their applications behave predictably and handle user interactions and system events gracefully.

The activity lifecycle consists of several distinct states, including:

Created: The activity has been created but is not yet visible to the user. In this state, the activity's onCreate() method is called, allowing developers to perform initialization tasks, such as inflating the layout, binding data, and setting up UI components.

javaCopy code

```
@Override protected void onCreate(Bundle savedInstanceState) { super.onCreate(savedInstanceState);
```

setContentView(R.layout.activity_main); // Perform initialization tasks here }

Started: The activity is visible to the user but may not be in the foreground or actively interacting with the user. In this state, the activity's onStart() method is called, allowing developers to perform tasks such as starting animations or loading data from external sources.

javaCopy code

@Override protected void onStart() { super.onStart(); // Perform tasks when the activity becomes visible }

Resumed: The activity is in the foreground and actively interacting with the user. In this state, the activity's onResume() method is called, allowing developers to start or resume tasks that require user interaction, such as playing media or updating UI elements.

javaCopy code

@Override protected void onResume() { super.onResume(); // Perform tasks when the activity is resumed }

Paused: The activity is partially obscured by another activity and no longer has focus, but is still visible to the user. In this state, the activity's onPause() method is called, allowing developers to pause ongoing tasks or save the activity's state.

javaCopy code

@Override protected void onPause() { super.onPause(); // Perform tasks when the activity is paused }

Stopped: The activity is no longer visible to the user and has been stopped. In this state, the activity's onStop() method is called, allowing developers to release resources or perform cleanup tasks.

javaCopy code

@Override protected void onStop() { super.onStop(); // Perform tasks when the activity is stopped }

Destroyed: The activity is being destroyed and is no longer in memory. In this state, the activity's onDestroy() method is called, allowing developers to release resources, unregister listeners, and perform final cleanup tasks.

javaCopy code

@Override protected void onDestroy() { super.onDestroy(); // Perform tasks when the activity is destroyed }

Understanding the activity lifecycle is crucial for handling configuration changes, such as screen rotations or changes in device orientation, which can cause the activity to be destroyed and recreated. By properly managing the activity's state and restoring its state during recreation, developers can ensure that users do not lose their progress or data when the configuration changes.

To handle configuration changes effectively, developers can use the onSaveInstanceState() and onRestoreInstanceState() methods to save and restore the activity's state, respectively. These methods allow developers to store key-value pairs of data in a Bundle object, which is preserved across configuration changes and can be used to restore the activity's state when it is recreated.

javaCopy code

@Override protected void onSaveInstanceState(Bundle outState) { super.onSaveInstanceState(outState); // Save the activity's state here } @Override protected void onRestoreInstanceState(Bundle savedInstanceState) { super.onRestoreInstanceState(savedInstanceState); // Restore the activity's state here }

In addition to handling configuration changes, developers must also consider other factors that can affect the activity lifecycle, such as the user navigating away from the activity, the system reclaiming resources, or the application being terminated by the user or the system. By understanding these factors and implementing appropriate lifecycle methods, developers can ensure that their applications respond appropriately to changes in the environment and provide a seamless user experience.

The activity lifecycle is a fundamental concept in Android development, and mastering it is essential for creating high-quality applications that meet the needs and expectations of users. By understanding the lifecycle states and callback methods, developers can effectively manage the behavior and state of their activities, handle configuration changes, and provide a seamless and responsive user experience across different devices and scenarios. With the right knowledge and skills, developers can leverage the activity lifecycle to create robust, reliable, and user-friendly applications that stand out in the competitive Android app market.

Intent usage and navigation are fundamental concepts in Android development, enabling developers to facilitate communication between different components of an application and navigate between various screens or activities seamlessly. Intents serve as a messaging mechanism that allows different components, such as activities, services, and broadcast receivers, to communicate with each other, either within the same application or across different applications. By understanding how to use intents effectively, developers can implement various functionalities, such as starting new activities, passing data between activities, and triggering actions or services, enhancing the functionality and usability of their applications.

In Android, intents are classified into two types: explicit intents and implicit intents. Explicit intents are used to start a specific component within the same application by specifying the target component's class name or package name. This type of intent is commonly used for internal navigation within an application, such as starting a new activity or launching a service.

To create an explicit intent and start a new activity, developers can use the Intent class and specify the target activity's class name using the setClass() or setComponent() method. For example:

javaCopy code

```
Intent intent = new Intent(MainActivity.this, SecondActivity.class); startActivity(intent);
```

In this example, an explicit intent is created to start the SecondActivity class from the MainActivity class. The startActivity() method is then called to initiate the navigation and switch to the target activity.

Another way to start an activity using an explicit intent is to specify the target activity's class name directly in the Intent constructor. For example:

javaCopy code

```
Intent intent = new Intent(MainActivity.this, SecondActivity.class); startActivity(intent);
```

In this case, the Intent constructor takes two parameters: the context (MainActivity.this) and the target activity's class name (SecondActivity.class).

Explicit intents can also be used to pass data between activities by adding extras to the intent before starting the target activity. Extras are key-value pairs of data that can be retrieved by the target activity using the getIntent().getExtras() method. For example:

javaCopy code

```
Intent intent = new Intent(MainActivity.this, SecondActivity.class); intent.putExtra("key", "value");
startActivity(intent);
```

In this example, a string value ("value") is passed to the target activity with the key "key". The target activity can retrieve this value using the getIntent().getStringExtra() method.

In addition to explicit intents, Android also supports implicit intents, which are used to trigger actions or start components based on their capabilities or the data they can handle. Implicit intents do not specify a specific target component but instead define an action to be performed, such as opening a web page, sending an email, or picking a contact from the device's contacts list. The system then resolves the intent and determines the appropriate component to handle the action based on its intent filters.

To create an implicit intent and perform an action, developers can specify the action to be performed using the setAction() method and add additional data or parameters as needed. For example:

javaCopy code

```
Intent intent = new Intent(Intent.ACTION_VIEW, Uri.parse("https://www.example.com"));
startActivity(intent);
```

In this example, an implicit intent is created to open a web page with the URL "https://www.example.com". The setAction() method is used to specify the action ACTION_VIEW, which instructs the system to view the content at the specified URI.

Implicit intents can also be used to start activities for actions such as sending emails, making phone calls, or sharing content with other applications. For example:

javaCopy code

```
Intent intent = new Intent(Intent.ACTION_SEND);
intent.setType( "text/plain" );
intent.putExtra(Intent.EXTRA_TEXT, "Check out this cool
app!" ); startActivity(Intent.createChooser(intent, "Share
via" ));
```

In this example, an implicit intent is created to send a plain text message using the ACTION_SEND action. The setType() method specifies the MIME type of the data to be sent, and the putExtra() method adds the text message to be shared. The startActivity() method is then called to start the activity for sending the message, and the createChooser() method is used to display a dialog allowing the user to choose from a list of available applications for sharing the content.

In addition to starting activities, intents can also be used to start services, broadcast messages, and perform other actions within an application. By understanding how to use both explicit and implicit intents effectively, developers can implement various functionalities and navigation patterns in their applications, providing a seamless and intuitive user experience.

Overall, intent usage and navigation are essential concepts in Android development, enabling developers to facilitate communication between different components of an application and navigate between various screens or activities seamlessly. By mastering the use of intents, developers can implement various functionalities, such as starting activities, passing data between components, and triggering actions or services, enhancing the functionality and usability of their applications. With the right knowledge and skills, developers can leverage intents to create powerful and intuitive Android applications that meet the needs and expectations of users.

Chapter 6: Managing Data with SQLite Databases

SQLite is a powerful and lightweight relational database management system that is widely used in various software applications, including mobile apps, desktop applications, and embedded systems. It is known for its simplicity, efficiency, and ease of integration, making it an ideal choice for developers who need a reliable and efficient database solution for their projects. SQLite is a self-contained, serverless, zero-configuration database engine that requires minimal setup and administration, making it easy to deploy and use in a wide range of environments.

One of the key features of SQLite is its simplicity and ease of use, which allows developers to create, read, update, and delete data using a simple and intuitive SQL-based interface. SQLite databases are stored as single files on disk, making them portable and easy to manage. Developers can interact with SQLite databases using standard SQL commands, such as SELECT, INSERT, UPDATE, and DELETE, to perform various operations on the data.

To create a new SQLite database file, developers can use the sqlite3 command-line tool, which comes pre-installed with most operating systems. By running the sqlite3 command followed by the desired database file name, developers can open a new or existing SQLite database and start executing SQL commands. For example, to create a new SQLite database file named "example.db," developers can use the following command:

bashCopy code

```
sqlite3 example.db
```

This command opens the SQLite command-line interface and creates a new SQLite database file named "example.db" in the current directory. Developers can then use SQL commands to create tables, insert data, and perform other operations on the database.

Once a SQLite database file is created, developers can use various tools and libraries to interact with the database programmatically from their applications. In Android development, for example, developers can use the SQLiteDatabase class provided by the Android SDK to create, open, and manage SQLite databases directly from their Java or Kotlin code. By using SQLiteDatabase methods such as insert(), update(), delete(), and query(), developers can perform CRUD (Create, Read, Update, Delete) operations on the database and manipulate the data as needed.

javaCopy code

```
// Create or open an existing SQLite database SQLiteDatabase database = SQLiteDatabase.openOrCreateDatabase( "example.db" , null ); // Create a new table database.execSQL( "CREATE TABLE IF NOT EXISTS users (id INTEGER PRIMARY KEY, name TEXT, email TEXT)" ); // Insert a new record into the table ContentValues values = new ContentValues (); values.put( "name" , "John Doe" ); values.put( "email" , "john@example.com" ); database.insert( "users" , null , values); // Query the database Cursor cursor = database.query( "users" , null , null , null , null , null , null ); // Iterate over the results if (cursor != null && cursor.moveToFirst()) { do { String name = cursor.getString(cursor.getColumnIndex( "name" )); String email = cursor.getString(cursor.getColumnIndex( "email" )); // Process the data as needed } while
```

(cursor.moveToNext()); cursor.close(); } // Close the database connection database.close();

In this example, a new SQLite database file named "example.db" is created or opened, and a new table named "users" is created if it does not already exist. A new record containing the name and email fields is then inserted into the "users" table using the insert() method. Subsequently, the database is queried using the query() method, and the results are retrieved using a Cursor object. Finally, the database connection is closed to release system resources.

SQLite is also commonly used in web development, particularly in combination with other technologies such as PHP, Python, and Node.js, to create dynamic and data-driven web applications. Developers can use SQLite with web frameworks such as Flask, Django, and Express.js to store and retrieve data from the database and render dynamic content to users.

In addition to its simplicity and ease of use, SQLite offers several other advantages, including reliability, scalability, and performance. SQLite databases are highly reliable and resilient to corruption, thanks to features such as atomic commit and rollback, which ensure data integrity and consistency. SQLite databases are also highly scalable and can handle large volumes of data efficiently, making them suitable for applications with varying data storage requirements. Furthermore, SQLite is optimized for performance, with features such as query optimization, indexing, and caching, which ensure fast and responsive data access.

Overall, SQLite is a versatile and powerful database management system that offers simplicity, reliability, and performance, making it an ideal choice for a wide range of applications and environments. Whether you're developing a mobile app, desktop application, or web application, SQLite provides a lightweight and efficient solution for storing and managing data. With its intuitive SQL-based interface, minimal setup requirements, and cross-platform compatibility, SQLite is an invaluable tool for developers looking to build robust and scalable software applications.

Database operations in Android are fundamental for developing robust and data-driven applications, empowering developers to store, retrieve, manipulate, and manage structured data efficiently. Android provides built-in support for SQLite, a lightweight and embedded relational database management system, which is widely used due to its simplicity, reliability, and performance. Leveraging SQLite, developers can implement various database operations seamlessly within their Android applications, ranging from creating and managing database schemas to performing CRUD (Create, Read, Update, Delete) operations on data records, enabling sophisticated data-driven functionalities.

To initiate database operations in Android, developers typically start by defining a SQLite database helper class that extends the SQLiteOpenHelper class provided by the Android SDK. This helper class encapsulates the logic for creating, upgrading, and managing the SQLite database, including defining the database schema and implementing methods for executing SQL statements and transactions. Using the SQLiteOpenHelper class, developers can ensure proper database initialization and version management, facilitating seamless database operations throughout the application's lifecycle.

javaCopy code

```
public class DatabaseHelper extends SQLiteOpenHelper { private static final String DATABASE_NAME =
```

"app_database.db"; private static final int DATABASE_VERSION = 1; public DatabaseHelper(Context context) { super(context, DATABASE_NAME, null, DATABASE_VERSION); } @Override public void onCreate(SQLiteDatabase db) { // Create database tables db.execSQL("CREATE TABLE IF NOT EXISTS users (id INTEGER PRIMARY KEY, name TEXT, email TEXT)"); } @Override public void onUpgrade(SQLiteDatabase db, int oldVersion, int newVersion) { // Upgrade database schema db.execSQL("DROP TABLE IF EXISTS users"); onCreate(db); }
}

In this example, a DatabaseHelper class is defined to manage the SQLite database named "app_database.db". The onCreate() method is overridden to create the database tables when the database is first created, and the onUpgrade() method is overridden to handle database schema upgrades by dropping and recreating the database tables.

Once the database helper class is defined, developers can use it to perform database operations within their Android application activities or other components. Common database operations include inserting, updating, deleting, and querying data records, which can be achieved using the SQLiteDatabase class provided by the Android SDK.

javaCopy code

public class MainActivity extends AppCompatActivity { private DatabaseHelper databaseHelper; @Override protected void onCreate(Bundle savedInstanceState) { super.onCreate(savedInstanceState);
setContentView(R.layout.activity_main); // Initialize database helper databaseHelper = new

```
DatabaseHelper(this); // Insert data into the database
insertUserData("John Doe", "john@example.com"); //
Query data from the database List<User> users = getUsers();
// Display user data for (User user : users) { Log.d("User",
"ID: " + user.getId() + ", Name: " + user.getName() + ",
Email: " + user.getEmail()); } } private void
insertUserData(String name, String email) { SQLiteDatabase
db = databaseHelper.getWritableDatabase();
ContentValues values = new ContentValues();
values.put("name", name); values.put("email", email);
db.insert("users", null, values); db.close(); } private
List<User> getUsers() { List<User> users = new
ArrayList<>(); SQLiteDatabase db =
databaseHelper.getReadableDatabase(); Cursor cursor =
db.query("users", null, null, null, null, null, null); if
(cursor != null && cursor.moveToFirst()) { do { int id =
cursor.getInt(cursor.getColumnIndex("id")); String name =
cursor.getString(cursor.getColumnIndex("name")); String
email = cursor.getString(cursor.getColumnIndex("email"));
users.add(new User(id, name, email)); } while
(cursor.moveToNext()); cursor.close(); } db.close(); return
users; } }
```

In this example, a MainActivity class is defined to demonstrate database operations within an Android activity. The DatabaseHelper instance is created in the onCreate() method to initialize the SQLite database. Data is inserted into the "users" table using the insertUserData() method, and then retrieved using the getUsers() method, which queries the database and populates a list of User objects.

Additionally, Android provides support for asynchronous database operations using the AsyncTask class or other concurrency mechanisms, allowing developers to perform database operations on background threads to prevent blocking the main UI thread and ensure a smooth user experience. By executing database operations asynchronously, developers can improve the responsiveness and performance of their Android applications, particularly when dealing with large datasets or complex queries.

Overall, database operations play a crucial role in Android development, enabling developers to implement sophisticated data-driven functionalities and provide seamless user experiences. By leveraging SQLite and the Android SDK's built-in database management capabilities, developers can create robust and efficient Android applications that effectively store, retrieve, and manage structured data, meeting the needs and expectations of users. With the right knowledge and skills, developers can leverage database operations to build powerful and feature-rich Android applications that stand out in the competitive mobile app market.

Chapter 7: Incorporating Images and Media into Your App

Loading and displaying images in Android applications is a fundamental task that developers frequently encounter, essential for creating visually appealing and engaging user interfaces. Android provides various techniques and libraries for efficiently loading and displaying images from local storage, network resources, or other external sources, catering to diverse use cases and requirements. By understanding these techniques and leveraging appropriate libraries, developers can ensure smooth and responsive image loading and rendering, enhancing the overall user experience of their applications.

One common approach to loading and displaying images in Android is using the built-in ImageView widget, which allows developers to display images within their application's user interface. To load an image into an ImageView, developers typically need to specify the image resource using the src attribute or programmatically set the image using the setImageResource(), setImageDrawable(), or setImageBitmap() methods. This approach is suitable for displaying static images bundled with the application or stored locally on the device.

xmlCopy code

```
<ImageView android:id="@+id/imageView"
android:layout_width="wrap_content"
android:layout_height="wrap_content"
android:src="@drawable/image_name" />
```

In this example, an ImageView widget is defined in an XML layout file, and the image resource "image_name" is specified using the src attribute. At runtime, Android automatically loads and displays the specified image in the

ImageView, providing a convenient way to display static images within the application.

Another common approach to loading and displaying images in Android is using the Glide library, a popular image loading and caching library developed by Google. Glide simplifies the process of loading and displaying images from various sources, such as URLs, URIs, file paths, or byte arrays, and provides features like image resizing, caching, and placeholder images, enhancing the performance and efficiency of image loading in Android applications.

To integrate Glide into an Android project, developers need to add the Glide dependency to their project's build.gradle file and then use the Glide library to load images into ImageView widgets or other image views within their application's layout files or code.

gradleCopy code

```
implementation 'com.github.bumptech.glide:glide:4.12.0'
annotationProcessor
'com.github.bumptech.glide:compiler:4.12.0'
```

Once the Glide library is added to the project, developers can use the Glide.with() method to initiate a new Glide request and specify the image source using the load() method. Additional options, such as resizing, transformations, and placeholder images, can be applied using method chaining, allowing developers to customize the image loading process according to their requirements.

javaCopy code

```
ImageView imageView = findViewById(R.id.imageView);
String imageUrl = "https://example.com/image.jpg";
Glide.with(this) .load(imageUrl)
.placeholder(R.drawable.placeholder)
.error(R.drawable.error) .centerCrop() .into(imageView);
```

In this example, Glide is used to load an image from a remote URL ("https://example.com/image.jpg") into an ImageView widget. Placeholder and error images are specified to display while the image is loading or in case of an error, and the centerCrop() method is used to resize and crop the image to fit the ImageView dimensions.

Additionally, Android provides support for loading and displaying images asynchronously using the AsyncTask class or other concurrency mechanisms. By performing image loading operations on background threads, developers can prevent blocking the main UI thread and ensure a smooth and responsive user experience, particularly when loading large or multiple images.

javaCopy code

```
class ImageLoaderTask extends AsyncTask<String, Void, Bitmap> { private ImageView imageView; public ImageLoaderTask(ImageView imageView) { this.imageView = imageView; } @Override protected Bitmap doInBackground(String... urls) { String imageUrl = urls[0]; try { URL url = new URL(imageUrl); HttpURLConnection connection = (HttpURLConnection) url.openConnection(); InputStream inputStream = connection.getInputStream(); return BitmapFactory.decodeStream(inputStream); } catch (IOException e) { e.printStackTrace(); return null; } } @Override protected void onPostExecute(Bitmap bitmap) { if (bitmap != null) { imageView.setImageBitmap(bitmap); } } } // Usage ImageView imageView = findViewById(R.id.imageView); String imageUrl = "https://example.com/image.jpg"; new ImageLoaderTask(imageView).execute(imageUrl);
```

In this example, an AsyncTask subclass is defined to load an image from a remote URL asynchronously. The doInBackground() method performs the image loading operation on a background thread, while the onPostExecute() method updates the ImageView with the loaded image on the main UI thread. By executing the ImageLoaderTask asynchronously, developers can prevent UI blocking and ensure a smooth image loading experience for users.

Overall, loading and displaying images in Android applications is a crucial aspect of creating visually appealing and engaging user interfaces. By leveraging techniques such as ImageView widgets, image loading libraries like Glide, and asynchronous image loading mechanisms, developers can efficiently load and display images from various sources, enhancing the user experience and usability of their applications. With the right knowledge and skills, developers can implement robust and efficient image loading functionalities that meet the needs and expectations of users.

Playing media files is a fundamental aspect of multimedia applications, allowing developers to incorporate audio and video content into their applications to enhance user experiences. In Android, developers can leverage various APIs and frameworks to implement media playback functionalities, supporting a wide range of media formats and playback controls. By understanding these techniques and APIs, developers can create immersive and interactive multimedia applications that cater to diverse user preferences and requirements.

One common approach to playing media files in Android is using the MediaPlayer class provided by the Android SDK, which offers built-in support for audio and video playback.

The MediaPlayer class provides methods for loading media files from local storage, network resources, or content providers, as well as controlling playback, handling playback state changes, and implementing various playback features such as looping, seeking, and volume control.
To play a media file using the MediaPlayer class, developers typically need to create a MediaPlayer instance, set the data source to the desired media file, prepare the media player for playback, and start or pause playback as needed. Additionally, developers can register callback listeners to receive notifications about playback state changes, errors, or completion events, allowing them to implement custom playback logic and user interactions.
javaCopy code

```
MediaPlayer mediaPlayer = new MediaPlayer(); try {
mediaPlayer.setDataSource("path_to_audio_file.mp3");
mediaPlayer.prepare(); mediaPlayer.start(); } catch
(IOException e) { e.printStackTrace(); }
```

In this example, a MediaPlayer instance is created, and the data source is set to the local path of an audio file ("path_to_audio_file.mp3"). The media player is then prepared for playback using the prepare() method and started using the start() method. If an IOException occurs during the setup process, it is caught and handled appropriately.
While the MediaPlayer class provides basic audio and video playback capabilities, it has certain limitations, such as lack of support for streaming media, limited customization options, and potential compatibility issues with specific media formats or devices. To overcome these limitations and implement more advanced media playback functionalities, developers can use third-party media playback libraries and frameworks, such as ExoPlayer and VLC for Android.

ExoPlayer, developed by Google, is a flexible and extensible media playback library for Android that offers advanced features such as adaptive streaming, dynamic buffering, and support for a wide range of media formats and protocols. ExoPlayer provides a modular architecture that allows developers to customize and extend its functionality through various components and extensions, enabling advanced media playback scenarios such as live streaming, DRM support, and seamless transitions between different media sources.

To integrate ExoPlayer into an Android project, developers need to add the ExoPlayer dependency to their project's build.gradle file and then use the ExoPlayer library to create a SimpleExoPlayer instance, set the media source to the desired media file or URI, and attach the player to a media player view for rendering.

gradleCopy code

```
implementation 'com.google.android.exoplayer:exoplayer-core:2.X.X' implementation 'com.google.android.exoplayer:exoplayer-ui:2.X.X'
```

javaCopy code

```
SimpleExoPlayer player = new SimpleExoPlayer .Builder(context).build(); MediaItem mediaItem = MediaItem.fromUri( "path_to_audio_file.mp3" ); player.setMediaItem(mediaItem); player.prepare(); player.play();
```

In this example, a SimpleExoPlayer instance is created using the SimpleExoPlayer.Builder class, and the media item is set to the local path of an audio file ("path_to_audio_file.mp3"). The player is then prepared for playback using the prepare() method and started using the play() method.

Alternatively, developers can use the ExoPlayerView widget provided by the ExoPlayer library to simplify the integration of ExoPlayer into their application's layout files and provide a consistent user interface for media playback. The ExoPlayerView widget encapsulates the logic for rendering media content and providing playback controls, allowing developers to focus on implementing playback logic and customizing the user interface according to their requirements.

xmlCopy code

```
<com.google.android.exoplayer2.ui.PlayerView
android:id="@+id/playerView"
android:layout_width="match_parent"
android:layout_height="wrap_content" />
```

javaCopy code

```
SimpleExoPlayer player = new SimpleExoPlayer.Builder(context).build(); PlayerView playerView = findViewById(R.id.playerView); playerView.setPlayer(player); MediaItem mediaItem = MediaItem.fromUri("path_to_audio_file.mp3"); player.setMediaItem(mediaItem); player.prepare(); player.play();
```

In this example, an ExoPlayerView widget is defined in an XML layout file, and the SimpleExoPlayer instance is attached to the player view using the setPlayer() method. The media item is then set to the local path of an audio file, and the player is prepared and started for playback.

Overall, playing media files in Android applications is essential for creating engaging and interactive user experiences, and developers can leverage various techniques and libraries to implement advanced media playback functionalities. Whether using the built-in MediaPlayer class for basic playback or integrating third-party libraries like

ExoPlayer for more advanced features, developers have a wide range of options available to meet the multimedia needs of their applications and users. With the right knowledge and skills, developers can create immersive and compelling multimedia applications that captivate and delight users across different devices and platforms.

Chapter 8: Introduction to Android Studio Layout Editor

The Layout Editor interface in Android Studio provides developers with a powerful and intuitive visual design tool for creating and editing user interface layouts for their Android applications. It offers a comprehensive set of features and tools that streamline the process of designing layouts, allowing developers to efficiently arrange UI components, define their properties, and visualize the layout's appearance on different devices and screen sizes. Understanding the Layout Editor interface is essential for developers to leverage its full potential and effectively design visually appealing and responsive user interfaces for their Android applications.

Upon opening a layout file in Android Studio, developers are presented with the Layout Editor interface, which consists of various panels, tools, and controls that facilitate layout design and customization. The Layout Editor interface is divided into several main sections, including the design surface, component tree, attributes panel, toolbar, and palette, each serving specific purposes in the layout design process.

The design surface is the central component of the Layout Editor interface, where developers can visually design and manipulate UI layouts using a WYSIWYG (What You See Is What You Get) approach. The design surface displays a real-time preview of the layout, allowing developers to interactively add, remove, and rearrange UI components by dragging and dropping them onto the canvas. Developers can also resize and position UI components directly on the design surface, using guidelines and snapping features to align components accurately.

The component tree panel, located on the left side of the Layout Editor interface, provides a hierarchical view of the UI components present in the layout. It lists all the components nested within the layout, organized in a tree structure according to their parent-child relationships. Developers can use the component tree to navigate the layout hierarchy, select and manipulate individual components, and view and edit their properties and attributes.

The attributes panel, situated on the right side of the Layout Editor interface, displays the properties and attributes of the selected UI component. It provides a convenient way for developers to modify the appearance and behavior of UI components by adjusting their properties, such as dimensions, margins, padding, colors, and text attributes. Developers can use the attributes panel to fine-tune the appearance of UI components and customize their behavior to meet specific design requirements.

The toolbar, located at the top of the Layout Editor interface, contains various tools and controls for managing layout design and editing operations. It includes buttons for common actions such as adding new UI components, aligning components, grouping and ungrouping components, and toggling between different layout editing modes. The toolbar also provides options for previewing the layout on different device configurations, enabling developers to assess the layout's responsiveness and adaptability to various screen sizes and orientations.

The palette, positioned on the left side of the Layout Editor interface, displays a collection of UI components and layout containers that developers can use to build their layouts. It includes a wide range of pre-defined components such as buttons, text views, image views, input fields, and layout containers such as linear layout, relative layout, constraint layout, and frame layout. Developers can drag and drop

components from the palette onto the design surface to add them to the layout, speeding up the layout design process and ensuring consistency in UI design.
In addition to the main sections mentioned above, the Layout Editor interface also includes various contextual menus, context actions, and keyboard shortcuts that developers can use to perform common layout editing tasks efficiently. Contextual menus provide quick access to frequently used commands and operations, while context actions offer options for modifying selected components based on their current state and context. Keyboard shortcuts enable developers to perform actions and navigate the Layout Editor interface using keyboard commands, enhancing productivity and workflow efficiency.
Overall, the Layout Editor interface in Android Studio is a versatile and feature-rich tool that empowers developers to design, edit, and visualize UI layouts for their Android applications effectively. By familiarizing themselves with the Layout Editor interface and mastering its features and tools, developers can create visually stunning and responsive user interfaces that enhance the usability and appeal of their Android applications. With its intuitive WYSIWYG design approach, comprehensive editing capabilities, and real-time previewing features, the Layout Editor interface is an indispensable asset for Android developers seeking to deliver high-quality and user-friendly applications to their audience.

Creating layouts and views is a fundamental aspect of Android app development, enabling developers to design the user interface (UI) of their applications to deliver engaging and intuitive user experiences. In Android, layouts are XML files that define the structure and appearance of UI elements, while views represent the individual UI components displayed on the screen, such as buttons, text fields, images, and containers. By understanding the principles of layout design and mastering the techniques for creating and customizing layouts and views, developers can build visually appealing and responsive interfaces that meet the needs and preferences of their users.

To create layouts and views in Android, developers primarily use XML (eXtensible Markup Language) markup language to define the structure and properties of UI elements. XML provides a hierarchical structure for organizing UI components within the layout, allowing developers to specify the size, position, appearance, and behavior of each component using XML attributes and properties. By leveraging XML layout files, developers can achieve a high degree of flexibility and customization in designing UI layouts for their applications.

The first step in creating a layout is to define the root layout container, which serves as the parent container for all other UI components within the layout. Android offers several types of layout containers, each with its own characteristics and usage scenarios, such as LinearLayout, RelativeLayout, ConstraintLayout, FrameLayout, and GridLayout. Developers can choose the appropriate layout container based on the desired UI arrangement and design requirements.

xmlCopy code

```
<?xml version="1.0" encoding="utf-8"?> <LinearLayout
xmlns:android="http://schemas.android.com/apk/res/andro
id" android:layout_width="match_parent"
android:layout_height="match_parent"
android:orientation="vertical"> <!-- UI components go here
--> </LinearLayout>
```

In this example, a LinearLayout is used as the root layout container, with its orientation set to "vertical" to arrange UI components in a vertical stack. Developers can add child views and other layout containers within the LinearLayout to create the desired UI layout structure.

Once the root layout container is defined, developers can add individual views and layout containers as child elements within the XML layout file, specifying their properties and attributes to customize their appearance and behavior. Each UI component is represented by a corresponding XML element, with attributes defining its properties such as size, margin, padding, background color, text content, and event handlers.

xmlCopy code

```
<Button android:id="@+id/button"
android:layout_width="wrap_content"
android:layout_height="wrap_content" android:text="Click
Me" android:layout_margin="16dp"/>
```

In this example, a Button view is added to the layout, with specified attributes for its width, height, text content, and margin. The "@" symbol followed by "+id/" indicates that the button has a unique identifier ("button") that can be referenced programmatically in the application code.

In addition to specifying UI components directly within the XML layout file, developers can also use the Android Studio Layout Editor tool to visually design and edit layouts. The Layout Editor provides a graphical interface for dragging and dropping UI components onto the design surface, arranging them visually, and adjusting their properties using intuitive controls and inspectors.

xmlCopy code

```
<androidx.constraintlayout.widget.ConstraintLayout
xmlns:android="http://schemas.android.com/apk/res/andro
id" xmlns:app="http://schemas.android.com/apk/res-auto"
android:layout_width="match_parent"
android:layout_height="match_parent"> <Button
```

```
android:id="@+id/button"
android:layout_width="wrap_content"
android:layout_height="wrap_content" android:text="Click
Me" app:layout_constraintStart_toStartOf="parent"
app:layout_constraintEnd_toEndOf="parent"
app:layout_constraintTop_toTopOf="parent"
app:layout_constraintBottom_toBottomOf="parent"
android:layout_margin="16dp"/>
</androidx.constraintlayout.widget.ConstraintLayout>
```

In this example, a ConstraintLayout is used as the root layout container, and a Button view is added to the layout using constraints to specify its position relative to the parent layout. Developers can interactively adjust the layout and view properties using the Layout Editor's visual tools and inspectors, providing a more intuitive and efficient way to create complex UI layouts.

Once the layout is defined, developers can integrate it into their Android application by referencing it from the appropriate activity or fragment class using setContentView() method or LayoutInflater. This inflates the layout XML file at runtime and displays it on the screen when the corresponding activity or fragment is launched.

javaCopy code

```
@Override protected void onCreate(Bundle
savedInstanceState) { super.onCreate(savedInstanceState);
setContentView(R.layout.activity_main); }
```

In this example, the activity_main.xml layout file is inflated and set as the content view for the MainActivity class using the setContentView() method. When the MainActivity is launched, the layout defined in activity_main.xml is displayed on the screen, allowing users to interact with the UI components as specified.

Overall, creating layouts and views is a crucial aspect of Android app development, enabling developers to design visually appealing and responsive user interfaces for their applications. By leveraging XML layout files, the Android Studio Layout Editor, and appropriate layout containers and views, developers can create rich and interactive UI layouts that enhance the usability and user experience of their applications. With a solid understanding of layout design principles and techniques, developers can create polished and user-friendly Android applications that resonate with their target audience and achieve their intended objectives.

Chapter 9: Debugging and Testing Your App

Identifying and fixing bugs is a critical aspect of software development, ensuring the reliability, stability, and functionality of applications. Bugs, also known as defects or issues, are unintended errors or flaws in the code that cause the application to behave unexpectedly, produce incorrect results, or crash. Detecting and resolving bugs promptly is essential for maintaining the quality of software products and delivering a positive user experience. In Android development, where applications run on a variety of devices with different configurations and operating system versions, the process of identifying and fixing bugs can be particularly challenging. However, with the right strategies, tools, and techniques, developers can effectively diagnose and address bugs in their Android applications, ensuring optimal performance and user satisfaction.

One common approach to identifying and fixing bugs in Android applications is through manual testing and debugging. Manual testing involves executing the application on physical or virtual devices, systematically exploring different features and functionalities, and observing its behavior for any unexpected or incorrect outcomes. By following predefined test cases and scenarios, testers can uncover potential bugs and inconsistencies in the application's behavior, such as UI glitches, functional errors, or performance issues. Once a bug is identified, developers can use debugging techniques to trace its root cause and implement appropriate fixes.

Android Studio provides comprehensive debugging tools and features that facilitate the process of identifying and fixing bugs in Android applications. The built-in debugger allows developers to inspect the application's runtime behavior, monitor variable values, and step through the code execution line by line to identify potential issues. Developers can set breakpoints at specific lines of code where they suspect the bug may be occurring, pause the execution of the application when the breakpoint is reached, and examine the program state to understand the cause of the bug.

To start the debugging process in Android Studio, developers can use the "Debug" configuration to run the application in debug mode, which enables the debugger and allows them to set breakpoints and inspect the application's runtime behavior. They can then use the "Run" menu or the shortcut "Shift + F9" to launch the application in debug mode and start the debugging session. Once the application is running, developers can use the "Debug" window to view the call stack, variables, and threads, and interactively debug the application's code.

In addition to manual testing and debugging, developers can leverage automated testing techniques to identify and fix bugs in their Android applications. Automated testing involves writing test scripts and cases that simulate user interactions and system behaviors, executing them automatically, and verifying the application's behavior against expected outcomes. Automated tests can cover a wide range of scenarios, including unit tests, integration tests, and UI tests, allowing developers to identify bugs early in the development process and ensure consistent behavior across different device configurations.

Android provides support for various testing frameworks and tools that developers can use to create and execute automated tests for their applications. For example, JUnit and Mockito are popular testing frameworks for writing and running unit tests, which focus on testing individual components or modules of the application in isolation. Espresso is a UI testing framework that allows developers to write automated tests for user interface interactions, such as clicking buttons, entering text, and validating UI elements' properties and states. Robolectric is another testing framework that provides support for running unit tests on Android applications without requiring a physical device or emulator, enabling faster test execution and feedback cycles.

To run automated tests in Android Studio, developers can use the built-in test runner and Gradle build system to execute test suites and generate test reports. They can define test configurations in the project's build.gradle file, specifying the test targets, dependencies, and execution parameters. Developers can then use the "Run" menu or Gradle commands to execute the tests, monitor the test execution progress, and view the test results in the "Run" window or HTML reports.

In addition to testing frameworks and tools, developers can also use logging and monitoring techniques to identify and diagnose bugs in their Android applications. Logging involves inserting log statements at strategic points in the code to record important information, such as variable values, method invocations, and error messages, during the application's runtime. Developers can use logging frameworks like Logcat to capture and view log output from the application in real-time, allowing them to identify abnormal behavior, errors, or exceptions that may indicate the presence of bugs.

To use Logcat for logging and debugging in Android Studio, developers can open the Logcat window from the "View" menu or use the shortcut "Alt + 6." They can then filter the log output by log level, tag, or process ID to focus on specific messages or events relevant to the debugging session.

Developers can also use the Log.d(), Log.i(), Log.w(), and Log.e() methods to write log messages with different severity levels and tags, allowing them to categorize and prioritize log output based on its importance and relevance to the debugging process.

Overall, identifying and fixing bugs in Android applications requires a systematic and proactive approach, combining manual testing, debugging, automated testing, logging, and monitoring techniques to detect and resolve issues effectively. By leveraging the tools, frameworks, and best practices available in Android development, developers can ensure the reliability, stability, and quality of their applications, delivering exceptional user experiences and maximizing user satisfaction. With continuous testing, monitoring, and improvement efforts, developers can minimize the impact of bugs and deliver software products that meet the highest standards of quality and performance.

Testing strategies in Android Studio play a crucial role in ensuring the quality, reliability, and performance of Android applications. With the wide variety of Android devices, operating system versions, and user scenarios, thorough testing is essential to identify and address potential issues and bugs that may arise during development. Android Studio provides developers with a comprehensive set of tools, frameworks, and techniques for implementing various testing strategies, including unit testing, integration testing, UI testing, and performance testing. By adopting effective testing strategies and practices, developers can improve the overall quality of their Android applications and deliver a seamless user experience to their audience.

Unit testing is a fundamental testing strategy in software development, focusing on testing individual components or units of code in isolation to ensure their correctness and functionality. In Android development, unit tests are typically written using JUnit, a popular testing framework for Java applications, and executed using the built-in testing support provided by Android Studio. Developers can create unit test classes for their Android application's Java and Kotlin code, defining test methods to validate the behavior of specific classes, methods, or functions.

To run unit tests in Android Studio, developers can use the Gradle build system to execute test tasks defined in the project's build.gradle file. They can run unit tests locally on their development machine using the "test" Gradle task or the "test" command in the terminal, which compiles the test code, executes the tests, and generates test reports with the results. Developers can also configure continuous integration (CI) pipelines to automatically run unit tests on code changes, ensuring that new code additions or modifications do not introduce regressions or break existing functionality.

Integration testing is another testing strategy in Android development, focusing on testing the interactions and integration points between different components or modules of the application to verify their interoperability and compatibility. Integration tests are typically written using frameworks like Mockito or Robolectric, which provide support for mocking dependencies, simulating external interactions, and verifying component interactions and behaviors.

To run integration tests in Android Studio, developers can use the Gradle build system to execute integration test tasks defined in the project's build.gradle file. They can run integration tests locally on their development machine using the "connectedAndroidTest" Gradle task or the "connectedAndroidTest" command in the terminal, which deploys the application to a connected device or emulator, executes the tests, and generates test reports with the results. Developers can also use the Android Test Orchestrator to run tests in isolated environments, ensuring that tests are executed reliably and consistently across different devices and configurations.

UI testing is a critical testing strategy in Android development, focusing on testing the user interface (UI) of the application to verify its appearance, behavior, and interactions. UI tests are typically written using frameworks like Espresso or UI Automator, which provide support for simulating user interactions, navigating through UI screens, and validating UI elements' properties and states.

To run UI tests in Android Studio, developers can use the Gradle build system to execute UI test tasks defined in the project's build.gradle file. They can run UI tests locally on their development machine using the "connectedAndroidTest" Gradle task or the "connectedAndroidTest" command in the terminal, which deploys the application to a connected device or emulator, executes the tests, and generates test reports with the results. Developers can also use the Android Test Orchestrator to run tests in parallel, speeding up the test execution process and providing faster feedback on UI changes and regressions.

Performance testing is an essential testing strategy in Android development, focusing on evaluating the application's performance, responsiveness, and resource usage under different conditions and scenarios. Performance tests can include stress testing, load testing, and endurance testing, which assess the application's behavior under heavy workloads, high user traffic, and prolonged usage periods.

To run performance tests in Android Studio, developers can use profiling and monitoring tools provided by Android Studio, such as the Android Profiler and CPU Profiler, to analyze the application's performance metrics, including CPU usage, memory usage, network activity, and battery consumption. They can use these tools to identify performance bottlenecks, memory leaks, and inefficiencies in the application's code and optimize it accordingly to improve its overall performance and responsiveness.

In addition to the testing strategies mentioned above, developers can also leverage other testing techniques and practices, such as code reviews, static analysis, and user acceptance testing, to ensure the quality and reliability of their Android applications. By adopting a comprehensive testing approach and integrating testing into the development process from the outset, developers can detect and address issues early, reduce the risk of defects and regressions, and deliver high-quality Android applications that meet the expectations and requirements of their users. With continuous testing and refinement, developers can iterate on their applications, address feedback and suggestions from users, and continually improve the overall quality and user experience of their Android applications.

Chapter 10: Publishing Your First App to the Google Play Store

App preparation for publication is a crucial step in the Android development lifecycle, ensuring that the application is ready for distribution to users through the Google Play Store or other distribution channels. This process involves a series of tasks and considerations, including finalizing the application's features and functionality, optimizing its performance and stability, complying with platform guidelines and policies, preparing marketing materials and assets, and testing the application thoroughly to ensure a seamless user experience. By following best practices and guidelines for app preparation, developers can maximize the chances of their application's success and ensure a smooth launch and deployment process.

One of the first steps in app preparation for publication is to ensure that the application meets the necessary technical and functional requirements for distribution on the Google Play Store. This includes verifying that the application's features and functionality are complete and fully implemented, and that it operates as expected on a wide range of devices and screen sizes. Developers can use Android Studio to build and test the application on different device configurations and emulators, ensuring compatibility and responsiveness across various platforms and form factors.

Once the application's features and functionality are finalized, developers need to optimize its performance and stability to deliver a smooth and responsive user experience. This involves identifying and addressing performance bottlenecks, memory leaks, and other issues that may affect the application's performance, such as excessive CPU or memory usage, slow rendering times, or crashes and freezes. Developers can use profiling and monitoring tools provided by Android Studio, such as the Android Profiler and CPU Profiler, to analyze the application's performance metrics and identify areas for improvement.

In addition to performance optimization, developers also need to ensure that the application complies with platform guidelines and policies, including the Google Play Developer Program Policies and the Android App Distribution Agreement. This includes adhering to content policies, such as restrictions on illegal or harmful content, as well as technical policies, such as requirements for app functionality, user interface design, and app behavior. Developers can review the Google Play Developer Console for guidance on compliance requirements and use the Play Console's Policy Center to address any policy violations or issues identified during the review process.

Another important aspect of app preparation for publication is the creation of marketing materials and assets to promote the application and attract users. This includes designing app icons, screenshots, and promotional graphics that accurately represent the application's features and functionality and appeal to the target audience. Developers can use design tools such as Adobe Photoshop or Sketch to create high-quality graphics and assets, ensuring that they meet the size and resolution requirements specified by the Google Play Store.

Once the application is finalized and all necessary preparations have been made, developers need to package the application for distribution and prepare it for submission to the Google Play Store. This involves generating a signed APK (Android Package) file containing the compiled code and resources of the application, as well as any necessary configuration files and assets. Developers can use the "assembleRelease" Gradle task in Android Studio to build and package the application for release, generating a signed APK file that is ready for distribution.

Before submitting the application to the Google Play Store, developers need to create a listing for the application in the Google Play Developer Console, providing information such as the application's title, description, category, and screenshots. They also need to set pricing and distribution options, such as whether the application will be free or paid, and in which countries it will be available for download. Once the listing is created, developers can upload the signed APK file to the Google Play Developer Console and submit the application for review.

After submission, the application will undergo a review process by the Google Play Store team to ensure compliance with platform guidelines and policies. This may include automated checks for technical issues and policy violations, as well as manual review by Google Play reviewers. Developers can monitor the review status and receive feedback on their application through the Google Play Developer Console, making any necessary revisions or updates based on the review feedback.

Once the application passes the review process, it will be published to the Google Play Store and made available for download to users worldwide. Developers can monitor the application's performance and user feedback through the Google Play Developer Console, analyzing metrics such as downloads, ratings, and reviews to track its success and identify areas for improvement. By continuously monitoring and updating the application based on user feedback and market trends, developers can ensure its long-term success and maintain a positive user experience.

Uploading to the Google Play Store is a critical step in the process of distributing an Android application to users worldwide, providing developers with a platform to reach millions of potential users and monetize their apps. The Google Play Store offers a streamlined and user-friendly interface for developers to publish their applications, allowing them to create listings, set pricing and distribution options, and manage updates and releases efficiently. By following best practices and guidelines for uploading to the Google Play Store, developers can ensure a smooth and successful publishing process and maximize the visibility and reach of their applications.

Before uploading an application to the Google Play Store, developers need to ensure that the application meets the necessary technical and content requirements specified by Google. This includes verifying that the application's features and functionality are complete and fully implemented, and that it complies with the Google Play Developer Program Policies and the Android App Distribution Agreement. Developers can review the Google Play Developer Console for guidance on compliance requirements and use the Play Console's Policy Center to address any policy violations or issues identified during the review process.

Once the application is ready for publication, developers need to prepare it for upload to the Google Play Store by packaging it into a signed APK (Android Package) file containing the compiled code and resources of the application, as well as any necessary configuration files and assets. To generate a signed APK file, developers can use the "assembleRelease" Gradle task in Android Studio, which builds and packages the application for release and generates a signed APK file that is ready for distribution.

After generating the signed APK file, developers need to create a listing for the application in the Google Play Developer Console, providing information such as the application's title, description, category, and screenshots. They also need to set pricing and distribution options, such as whether the application will be free or paid, and in which countries it will be available for download. Developers can use the Google Play Developer Console to upload the signed APK file and any necessary assets, such as app icons, screenshots, and promotional graphics, to create a complete listing for the application.

Once the listing is created, developers can review and finalize the application's details, ensuring that all information is accurate and up-to-date. They can then submit the application for review to the Google Play Store team, who will evaluate the application to ensure compliance with platform guidelines and policies. The review process may include automated checks for technical issues and policy violations, as well as manual review by Google Play reviewers. Developers can monitor the review status and receive feedback on their application through the Google Play Developer Console, making any necessary revisions or updates based on the review feedback.

After the application passes the review process, it will be published to the Google Play Store and made available for download to users worldwide. Developers can monitor the application's performance and user feedback through the Google Play Developer Console, analyzing metrics such as downloads, ratings, and reviews to track its success and identify areas for improvement. They can also manage updates and releases of the application through the Play Console, uploading new versions of the APK file and updating the application's listing with new features, bug fixes, and improvements.

Throughout the lifecycle of the application, developers can use the Google Play Developer Console to manage various aspects of the application's distribution and performance, including app releases, pricing and distribution options, user feedback and reviews, and financial reports and earnings. By regularly monitoring and updating the application based on user feedback and market trends, developers can ensure its long-term success and maintain a positive user experience on the Google Play Store.

In summary, uploading to the Google Play Store is a critical step in the process of distributing an Android application to users worldwide, providing developers with a platform to reach millions of potential users and monetize their apps. By following best practices and guidelines for uploading to the Google Play Store, developers can ensure a smooth and successful publishing process and maximize the visibility and reach of their applications.

BOOK 2

ADVANCED ANDROID DEVELOPMENT TECHNIQUES

MASTERING ANDROID STUDIO

ROB BOTWRIGHT

Chapter 1: Advanced UI Design Patterns and Custom Views

Custom View Creation Techniques encompass a wide array of methods and strategies aimed at designing and implementing unique user interfaces tailored to specific needs and preferences. These techniques are essential in software development, enabling developers to create visually appealing and functional interfaces that enhance user experience and streamline workflow. From simple modifications to complex customization, custom view creation techniques offer developers the flexibility and creativity necessary to produce outstanding applications across various platforms and devices.

One fundamental approach to custom view creation is through the utilization of XML layouts combined with programmatically defined views. XML layouts provide a structured and declarative way to define the structure and appearance of user interfaces. Developers can leverage XML attributes to specify various properties such as dimensions, colors, and alignment, thus allowing for quick and efficient customization. Complementing XML layouts with programmatically defined views enables developers to dynamically adjust the layout and behavior of views based on runtime conditions and user interactions. This approach offers a high degree of flexibility and control over the user interface, empowering developers to create dynamic and interactive experiences.

Another common technique in custom view creation is the use of custom view classes. Custom view classes extend existing view classes provided by the Android framework, allowing developers to create specialized views tailored to their application's specific requirements. By subclassing view classes such as ViewGroup or View, developers can define custom drawing logic, handle touch events, and implement custom animations. This approach is particularly useful for creating complex or highly specialized user interface elements that cannot be achieved using standard views alone. To deploy this technique, developers can create a new Java class that extends the desired view class, override relevant methods to implement custom behavior, and then use the custom view in XML layouts or programmatically within their application code.

Furthermore, custom view creation techniques often involve the use of advanced graphics and animation APIs to enhance the visual appeal and interactivity of user interfaces. Techniques such as canvas drawing, custom animations, and shader effects allow developers to create visually stunning and immersive experiences that captivate users' attention. By leveraging the powerful graphics capabilities of the Android platform, developers can implement custom visual effects, transitions, and animations that elevate their applications to the next level. To implement custom graphics and animations, developers can use the Android Canvas API to draw custom shapes, text, and images directly onto the screen, or utilize the animation framework to create complex motion effects and transitions. Additionally, developers can take advantage of third-party libraries and tools to simplify the implementation of advanced graphics and animation effects, further accelerating the development process.

In addition to graphical customization, custom view creation techniques also encompass strategies for optimizing performance and responsiveness. Efficient layout management, view recycling, and asynchronous loading are crucial considerations for ensuring smooth and fluid user experiences, especially in applications with large or dynamic user interfaces. Techniques such as RecyclerView for efficient list and grid layouts, ConstraintLayout for flexible and responsive designs, and AsyncTask for background task execution are commonly employed to optimize performance and responsiveness. By adopting these techniques, developers can ensure that their applications deliver a seamless and responsive user experience across a wide range of devices and usage scenarios.

Moreover, accessibility and internationalization are essential aspects of custom view creation that should not be overlooked. Ensuring that user interfaces are accessible to users with disabilities and are localized for different languages and regions is critical for reaching a diverse audience and providing an inclusive user experience. Techniques such as providing alternative text for images, using system-provided text scaling, and supporting right-to-left layouts are essential for improving accessibility and internationalization. Developers can leverage platform features such as accessibility services and resource qualifiers to implement accessibility and internationalization features effectively. Additionally, testing with assistive technologies and diverse user groups is essential for validating the accessibility and internationalization of custom views and ensuring compliance with accessibility standards and best practices.

Furthermore, custom view creation techniques extend beyond traditional graphical user interfaces to encompass emerging paradigms such as voice interfaces, augmented reality, and wearable devices. Voice-enabled interfaces allow users to interact with applications using natural language commands, opening up new possibilities for hands-free interaction and accessibility. Techniques such as speech recognition and natural language processing enable developers to create voice-enabled interfaces that understand and respond to user input effectively. Augmented reality interfaces overlay digital content onto the physical world, creating immersive and interactive experiences that blend virtual and real environments. Techniques such as marker detection, object tracking, and spatial mapping enable developers to create augmented reality applications that enhance user engagement and interaction. Wearable devices such as smartwatches and fitness trackers offer new opportunities for creating custom user interfaces tailored to the unique form factors and usage patterns of wearable devices. Techniques such as designing glanceable interfaces, optimizing for touch and voice input, and leveraging sensor data enable developers to create compelling user experiences for wearable devices.

In summary, custom view creation techniques play a vital role in software development, enabling developers to create unique and engaging user interfaces that enhance user experience and drive user engagement. By leveraging XML layouts, custom view classes, advanced graphics and animation APIs, performance optimization strategies, accessibility and internationalization techniques, and emerging interface paradigms, developers can create applications that stand out in today's competitive marketplace. By embracing creativity, innovation, and user-centric design principles, developers can unlock the full potential of custom view creation techniques to deliver outstanding applications that delight and inspire users.

Implementing Advanced UI Design Patterns involves the application of sophisticated design principles and techniques to create user interfaces that are intuitive, visually appealing, and efficient. These patterns go beyond basic layouts and styling, focusing on architectural concepts, interaction design, and user experience optimization to deliver exceptional software interfaces. One prominent pattern is the Model-View-ViewModel (MVVM), which facilitates separation of concerns and promotes maintainability and testability. In MVVM, the model represents the application data and business logic, the view displays the user interface elements, and the view model serves as an intermediary between the view and the model, handling user interactions and updating the view accordingly. To implement MVVM, developers can use frameworks such as Android Architecture Components or third-party libraries like RxJava to manage data binding and reactive programming, ensuring seamless communication between components.

Another essential pattern in advanced UI design is the use of dependency injection to manage object dependencies and facilitate modularization and unit testing. Dependency injection frameworks such as Dagger or Koin enable developers to define dependencies at compile time and inject them into objects at runtime, reducing coupling and promoting code reusability. To implement dependency injection, developers can define modules to provide dependencies and annotate classes with injection annotations to specify dependencies to be injected. By adopting dependency injection, developers can improve the maintainability, scalability, and testability of their codebase, making it easier to manage and evolve over time.

Moreover, advanced UI design patterns often involve the use of reactive programming techniques to handle asynchronous operations and manage complex UI state. Reactive programming frameworks such as RxJava or Kotlin Flow allow developers to model UI interactions as streams of data and apply operators to transform, filter, and combine these streams, enabling concise and expressive code. To implement reactive programming, developers can use observables to represent asynchronous data streams, subscribe to these streams to receive updates, and apply operators to manipulate the data as needed. By embracing reactive programming, developers can create responsive and interactive user interfaces that adapt to user input and external events, enhancing the overall user experience.

Additionally, advanced UI design patterns include the adoption of architectural patterns such as the Clean Architecture or the Flux architecture to structure and organize code in a clear and maintainable manner. Clean Architecture emphasizes separation of concerns and dependency inversion, with layers such as domain, data, and presentation, each responsible for specific aspects of the application. Flux architecture, popularized by libraries like Redux, introduces a unidirectional data flow model, where actions trigger state updates, which in turn propagate changes to the UI. To implement Clean Architecture, developers can define domain models and use cases in the domain layer, implement data access logic in the data layer, and implement UI logic in the presentation layer. To implement Flux architecture, developers can define actions to represent user interactions, reducers to update state based on actions, and components to render UI based on state. By adopting these architectural patterns, developers can create scalable, maintainable, and testable codebases that are easy to understand and evolve.

Furthermore, advanced UI design patterns encompass strategies for optimizing performance and responsiveness, such as lazy loading, caching, and prefetching data to minimize latency and improve user experience. Lazy loading involves loading data or resources on demand rather than upfront, reducing initial load times and conserving memory. Caching involves storing frequently accessed data locally to avoid repeated network requests and improve responsiveness. Prefetching involves anticipating user actions and proactively fetching data or resources in the background to minimize perceived latency. To implement these strategies, developers can use techniques such as pagination, memoization, and asynchronous loading to manage data retrieval and presentation efficiently. By optimizing performance and responsiveness, developers can ensure that their applications deliver a smooth and seamless user experience, even under challenging network conditions or resource constraints.

Moreover, advanced UI design patterns include techniques for implementing complex user interface components, such as custom views, gestures, and animations, to create engaging and interactive experiences. Custom views allow developers to create reusable UI components with custom appearance and behavior tailored to specific requirements. Gestures enable users to interact with the application through touch, swipe, pinch, and other intuitive gestures, enhancing usability and interactivity. Animations provide visual feedback and enhance the user experience by adding polish and delight to the interface. To implement these techniques, developers can use platform APIs such as Canvas and MotionEvent to create custom views and handle touch events, or use animation frameworks such as Lottie or MotionLayout to implement complex animations and transitions. By incorporating custom views, gestures, and animations into their applications, developers can create immersive and delightful user experiences that stand out in today's competitive marketplace.

In summary, implementing advanced UI design patterns requires a deep understanding of design principles, architectural concepts, and platform capabilities. By adopting patterns such as MVVM, dependency injection, reactive programming, and architectural patterns like Clean Architecture and Flux, developers can create software interfaces that are robust, maintainable, and responsive. Additionally, by optimizing performance and responsiveness, implementing complex user interface components, and embracing emerging technologies and trends, developers can create user experiences that delight and inspire users. By continually refining and evolving their design practices, developers can stay ahead of the curve and deliver outstanding applications that meet the needs and expectations of today's users.

Chapter 2: Working with Fragments for Flexible User Interfaces

Fragment Lifecycle Management is a critical aspect of Android app development, governing the creation, destruction, and state persistence of fragments, which are modular UI components that represent a portion of a user interface or behavior within an activity. Understanding the fragment lifecycle is essential for ensuring proper handling of UI state, resource management, and user interaction in Android applications. The fragment lifecycle consists of several key states, including the initial creation, starting, resuming, pausing, stopping, and destroying of fragments, each of which corresponds to specific callback methods that developers can override to customize behavior and respond to lifecycle events. One important aspect of fragment lifecycle management is ensuring that fragments are properly instantiated and attached to their parent activity, typically through XML layout files or programmatically within activity code. To create and add a fragment to an activity, developers can use the FragmentManager class to begin a transaction, specify the container view where the fragment will be placed, and commit the transaction to apply the changes. Additionally, developers can define custom constructors or factory methods in fragment classes to pass arguments or initialize dependencies when instantiating fragments, allowing for greater flexibility and reusability.

As fragments transition through their lifecycle states, they may need to perform various tasks such as initializing UI components, loading data from a network or database, or saving and restoring instance state to preserve user input and configuration changes. To handle these tasks, developers can override lifecycle callback methods such as onCreate(), onCreateView(), onViewCreated(), onStart(), onResume(), onPause(), onStop(), and onDestroy() to execute code at specific points in the fragment lifecycle. For example, the onCreateView() method is used to inflate the fragment's layout from a resource XML file and initialize UI components, while the onResume() method is typically used to resume ongoing tasks or update the UI after the fragment becomes visible to the user. By carefully managing fragment lifecycles and implementing lifecycle callback methods, developers can ensure that fragments behave predictably and maintain a consistent state throughout the lifetime of the application.

Another important aspect of fragment lifecycle management is handling configuration changes such as screen rotations, device orientation changes, or changes in system configuration (e.g., language or theme changes). During configuration changes, the activity hosting the fragment may be destroyed and recreated, causing all fragments to be recreated and their state to be lost if not properly handled. To preserve fragment state across configuration changes, developers can use techniques such as retaining fragments, saving and restoring instance state, or using ViewModel objects to store and manage UI-related data independently of the fragment lifecycle. Retaining fragments involves setting the setRetainInstance() method to true, which instructs the system to retain the fragment instance during configuration changes instead of destroying and recreating it. Alternatively, developers can override the onSaveInstanceState() and onViewStateRestored() methods to save and restore fragment state manually, typically by storing data in a Bundle object and retrieving it when the fragment is recreated. Additionally, developers can use ViewModel objects from the Android Architecture

Components library to store UI-related data in a lifecycle-aware manner, ensuring that data persists across configuration changes and is automatically cleaned up when the associated fragment or activity is destroyed.

Furthermore, fragment lifecycle management includes handling back stack behavior and fragment transactions to navigate between different fragments within an activity or across multiple activities. Fragments can be added to a back stack by calling the addToBackStack() method when committing a fragment transaction, allowing users to navigate back to previous fragments using the device's back button or programmatically within the application. To navigate between fragments, developers can use methods such as replace(), add(), or remove() to add, replace, or remove fragments from the activity's fragment container, and then commit the transaction to apply the changes. Additionally, developers can use the popBackStack() method to navigate back to a specific fragment or pop all fragments from the back stack until a specified destination is reached. By managing the back stack and fragment transactions effectively, developers can create intuitive and seamless navigation experiences that enhance user engagement and usability.

Moreover, fragment lifecycle management extends to handling communication and interaction between fragments and their parent activity or other fragments within the same activity. Fragments can communicate with their parent activity through callback interfaces or by accessing activity methods and properties directly. Additionally, fragments can communicate with other fragments within the same activity by obtaining references to each other through the FragmentManager or by using shared view models to share data between fragments. To implement communication between fragments, developers can define callback interfaces in fragment classes and implement them in the parent activity, allowing fragments to notify the activity of user actions or events. Alternatively, developers can use the setTargetFragment() and getTargetFragment() methods to establish communication between fragments directly, passing data or triggering actions between fragments as needed. By implementing effective communication patterns between fragments, developers can create cohesive and interconnected user interfaces that provide a seamless and intuitive user experience.

In summary, fragment lifecycle management is a fundamental aspect of Android app development that governs the creation, destruction, and state persistence of fragments within an activity. By understanding the fragment lifecycle and implementing lifecycle callback methods, developers can ensure that fragments behave predictably and maintain a consistent state throughout the lifetime of the application. Additionally, by handling configuration changes, managing back stack behavior and fragment transactions, and facilitating communication between fragments, developers can create robust and responsive user interfaces that enhance user engagement and usability. By mastering fragment lifecycle management techniques, developers can create high-quality Android applications that meet the needs and expectations of today's users.

Building Dynamic UIs with Fragments involves leveraging the versatility and flexibility of fragments, which are modular components in Android applications that encapsulate UI and behavior, to create dynamic and responsive user interfaces that adapt to various screen sizes, orientations, and configurations. Fragments offer a powerful way to design flexible and reusable UI components that can be combined and arranged dynamically within activities to accommodate different use cases and user interactions. One key aspect of building dynamic UIs with fragments is understanding how to dynamically add, remove, and replace fragments within an activity's layout to create rich and interactive user experiences. This can be achieved using the FragmentManager class, which provides methods for managing fragments programmatically, such as getSupportFragmentManager() to obtain a reference to the FragmentManager instance associated with the activity, and beginTransaction() to start a new fragment transaction.

To dynamically add a fragment to an activity's layout, developers can use the add() method to specify the container view ID where the fragment will be placed and the fragment instance to be added, and then commit the transaction to apply the changes. Similarly, to remove a fragment from the activity's layout, developers can use the remove() method to specify the fragment instance to be removed and commit the transaction. Additionally, developers can use the replace() method to replace an existing fragment with a new fragment instance, providing greater flexibility and control over the UI composition. By leveraging these methods, developers can create dynamic UIs that respond to user actions, such as navigation events or configuration changes, by adding, removing, or replacing fragments as needed.

Another important aspect of building dynamic UIs with fragments is understanding how to pass data between fragments and communicate with the parent activity or other fragments within the same activity. Fragments can communicate with their parent activity through callback interfaces or by accessing activity methods and properties directly. Additionally, fragments can communicate with other fragments within the same activity by obtaining references to each other through the FragmentManager or by using shared view models to share data between fragments. To implement communication between fragments, developers can define callback interfaces in fragment classes and implement them in the parent activity, allowing fragments to notify the activity of user actions or events. Alternatively, developers can use the setTargetFragment() and getTargetFragment() methods to establish communication between fragments directly, passing data or triggering actions between fragments as needed. By implementing effective communication patterns between fragments, developers can create cohesive and interconnected user interfaces that provide a seamless and intuitive user experience.

Moreover, building dynamic UIs with fragments involves designing responsive layouts that adapt to different screen sizes, orientations, and configurations. Fragments can be combined and arranged dynamically within activities to create layouts that scale gracefully across various devices and form factors. To design responsive layouts with fragments, developers can use techniques such as fragment nesting, where fragments are nested within other fragments to create hierarchical UI structures, or fragment transactions, where fragments are added, removed, or replaced dynamically based on runtime conditions. Additionally, developers can use layout managers such as LinearLayout, RelativeLayout, or ConstraintLayout to create flexible and adaptive UI designs that adjust to changes in screen size or orientation. By designing responsive layouts with fragments, developers can ensure that their applications provide a consistent and optimized user experience across a wide range of devices and usage scenarios.

Furthermore, building dynamic UIs with fragments involves managing fragment lifecycles and handling configuration changes to ensure that UI state is preserved and restored properly. During configuration changes such as screen rotations or device orientation changes, the activity hosting the fragments may be destroyed and recreated, causing all fragments to be recreated and their state to be lost if not properly handled. To preserve fragment state across configuration changes, developers can use techniques such as retaining fragments, saving and restoring instance state, or using ViewModel objects to store and manage UI-related data independently of the fragment lifecycle. Retaining fragments involves setting the setRetainInstance() method to true, which instructs the system to retain the fragment instance during configuration changes instead of destroying and recreating it. Alternatively, developers can override the onSaveInstanceState() and onViewStateRestored() methods to save and restore fragment state manually, typically by storing data in a Bundle object and retrieving it when the fragment is recreated. Additionally, developers can use ViewModel objects from the Android Architecture Components library to store UI-related data in a lifecycle-aware manner, ensuring that data persists across configuration changes and is automatically cleaned up when the associated fragment or activity is destroyed.

In summary, building dynamic UIs with fragments is a powerful approach to creating flexible and responsive user interfaces in Android applications. By leveraging the versatility of fragments, developers can design modular and reusable UI components that adapt to various screen sizes, orientations, and configurations, providing a consistent and optimized user experience across different devices and form factors. By understanding how to dynamically add, remove, and replace fragments within activities, how to pass data between fragments and communicate with the parent activity or other fragments, and how to manage fragment lifecycles and handle configuration changes effectively, developers can create rich and interactive user interfaces that meet the needs and expectations of today's users. With careful planning and implementation, building dynamic UIs with fragments can lead to the development of robust and scalable Android applications that stand out in today's competitive marketplace.

Chapter 3: Implementing Advanced Animation and Transition Effects

Animation APIs Overview provides an in-depth exploration of the various animation frameworks and libraries available for creating dynamic and engaging user interfaces in software applications across different platforms. Animation plays a crucial role in enhancing user experience by adding fluidity, responsiveness, and visual feedback to user interactions, thereby making applications more intuitive and appealing. One of the fundamental animation APIs widely used in web development is CSS Animations and Transitions, which allow developers to animate HTML elements using declarative CSS syntax. With CSS Animations, developers can define keyframes specifying the animation's start and end states, along with intermediate steps, and apply them to elements using the animation property. Transitions, on the other hand, enable smooth transitions between different CSS property values over a specified duration, making it easy to create effects such as fading, sliding, or scaling elements in response to user interactions or events.

Additionally, the Web Animations API provides a JavaScript-based interface for creating and controlling animations in web applications. The Web Animations API offers more flexibility and control over animations compared to CSS Animations and Transitions, allowing developers to create complex animations with fine-grained control over timing, easing, and playback. With the Web Animations API, developers can programmatically create animations, manipulate animation properties dynamically, and synchronize multiple animations to create seamless and interactive user experiences. To use the Web Animations API, developers can create animation objects using the Animation constructor, specify animation properties such as duration, timing function, and delay, and apply them to elements using the animate() method, which returns an Animation object representing the animation.

In the realm of mobile app development, Android provides a comprehensive set of animation APIs for creating animations and transitions in Android applications. One of the core animation frameworks in Android is the View Animation framework, which allows developers to animate the properties of UI elements such as views and layouts using XML-based animation resources. With View Animation, developers can define animations such as fading, scaling, rotating, or translating views by specifying the desired animation properties in XML files and applying them to views using the startAnimation() method. View Animation is well-suited for simple animations and transitions but has limitations in terms of performance and flexibility compared to more advanced animation frameworks available in Android.

For more complex animations and interactions, Android offers the Property Animation framework, which provides a more flexible and powerful API for animating arbitrary properties of objects in Android applications. With Property Animation, developers can animate not only visual properties such as alpha, scale, rotation, and translation but also custom properties of objects, enabling a wide range of creative and dynamic effects. Property Animation introduces the concept of animators and animator sets, which allow developers to define animations programmatically and apply them to objects using the animate() method. Additionally, Property Animation supports advanced features such as interpolators, which define the rate of change of an animation over time, and animators listeners, which allow developers to listen for animation events such as start, end, or repeat.

Furthermore, Android offers the Animated Vector Drawable framework, which allows developers to create complex vector-based animations using scalable vector graphics (SVG) files. Animated Vector Drawables enable developers to define animated vector graphics using XML-based vector drawable resources and animate them using the VectorDrawableCompat class. With Animated Vector Drawables, developers can create animations such as morphing, rotation, and scaling of vector graphics, making it easy to create visually appealing and interactive user interfaces in Android applications.

In addition to platform-specific animation frameworks, there are also cross-platform animation libraries and tools available for creating animations in web and mobile applications. One popular animation library is GreenSock Animation Platform (GSAP), which provides a comprehensive set of tools and APIs for creating high-performance animations in web applications using JavaScript. GSAP offers advanced features such as timeline sequencing, physics-based animations, and SVG morphing, making it a powerful tool for creating complex and interactive animations. To use GSAP, developers can include the GSAP library in their web projects using a script tag and use its API to create and control animations programmatically.

Moreover, there are several animation libraries and frameworks available for creating animations in mobile applications, such as Lottie, which allows developers to render Adobe After Effects animations in real-time using native animation APIs on Android and iOS. Lottie enables designers to create rich and expressive animations in After Effects and export them as JSON files that can be easily integrated into mobile applications using the Lottie library. To use Lottie, developers can include the Lottie library in their mobile projects using dependency management tools such as Gradle or CocoaPods and use the LottieAnimationView class to render animations in their applications.

In summary, Animation APIs Overview provides a comprehensive overview of the various animation frameworks and libraries available for creating dynamic and engaging animations in web and mobile applications. From CSS Animations and Transitions to the Web Animations API, View Animation, Property Animation, and Animated Vector Drawables in Android, to cross-platform animation libraries such as GSAP and Lottie, developers have a wide range of tools and technologies at their disposal for creating immersive and interactive animations. By understanding the capabilities and features of different animation APIs, developers can choose the right tools for their projects and create animations that enhance user experience and bring their applications to life.

Creating Complex Transition Effects involves leveraging

various animation techniques and libraries to achieve smooth, captivating transitions between different states or elements in software applications. These transitions play a crucial role in enhancing user experience, providing visual feedback, and guiding users through the interface with fluid and intuitive animations. One approach to creating complex transition effects is through the use of CSS transitions and animations in web development. CSS transitions allow developers to animate changes to CSS properties over a specified duration, enabling smooth transitions between different states or styles. To create a CSS transition, developers can define the initial and final states of an element using CSS selectors and then specify the transition properties such as duration, timing function, and delay using the transition property. For example, the following CSS code creates a transition effect for the color property of a button element:

cssCopy code

```
.button { color: blue; transition: color 0.3s ease; }
.button:hover { color: red; }
```

In this example, when the user hovers over the button element, the color transitions from blue to red over a duration of 0.3 seconds with an easing function applied for smooth acceleration and deceleration.

Additionally, CSS animations provide a more powerful and flexible way to create complex transition effects by defining keyframes specifying intermediate states of an animation. To create a CSS animation, developers can define keyframes using the @keyframes rule and then apply the animation to an element using the animation property. For example, the following CSS code creates a pulse animation for a button element:

cssCopy code

```css
@keyframes pulse { 0% { transform: scale(1); } 50% { transform: scale(1.1); } 100% { transform: scale(1); } } .button { animation: pulse 1s infinite alternate; }
```

In this example, the pulse animation scales the button element up and down infinitely with an alternate direction every second.

Another approach to creating complex transition effects is through the use of JavaScript animation libraries such as GreenSock Animation Platform (GSAP) or Anime.js. These libraries provide powerful APIs and features for creating advanced animations and transitions in web applications with cross-browser compatibility and optimal performance. GSAP, in particular, offers a comprehensive set of tools and plugins for creating complex animations, timelines, and motion effects. To use GSAP, developers can include the GSAP library in their web projects using a script tag and then use its API to create animations programmatically. For example, the following JavaScript code creates a fade-in animation for a button element using GSAP:

javascriptCopy code

```javascript
gsap.to('.button', { opacity: 1, duration: 1, ease: 'power2.out' });
```

In this example, the GSAP.to() method animates the opacity property of the button element from 0 to 1 over a duration of 1 second with a custom easing function applied for smooth acceleration.

Furthermore, creating complex transition effects in mobile app development involves leveraging platform-specific animation frameworks and libraries such as the Android Animation framework or the Core Animation framework in iOS. These frameworks provide APIs for creating animations and transitions in native Android and iOS applications, enabling developers to achieve smooth and responsive user interfaces. In Android, developers can use the View Animation framework or the more advanced Property Animation framework to create animations for UI elements such as views and layouts. For example, the following Java code creates a fade-in animation for a button element in Android:

javaCopy code

```java
ObjectAnimator fadeIn = ObjectAnimator.ofFloat(button, "alpha", 0f, 1f); fadeIn.setDuration(1000); fadeIn.start();
```

In this example, the ObjectAnimator class animates the alpha property of the button element from 0 to 1 over a duration of 1 second.

Similarly, in iOS, developers can use Core Animation to create animations and transitions for UI elements such as views and layers. For example, the following Swift code creates a fade-in animation for a button element in iOS:

swiftCopy code

```swift
UIView.animate(withDuration: 1.0) { button.alpha = 1.0
}
```

In this example, the UIView.animate(withDuration:) method animates the alpha property of the button element from 0 to 1 over a duration of 1 second.

In summary, creating complex transition effects involves leveraging various animation techniques and libraries to achieve smooth, captivating transitions between different states or elements in software applications. Whether through CSS transitions and animations in web development, JavaScript animation libraries such as GSAP, or platform-specific animation frameworks in mobile app development, developers have a wide range of tools and techniques at their disposal for creating immersive and engaging user interfaces. By understanding the capabilities and features of different animation techniques and libraries, developers can create visually stunning and interactive transition effects that enhance user experience and bring their applications to life.

Chapter 4: Handling Background Tasks with AsyncTask and AsyncTaskLoader

AsyncTask Implementation for Background Tasks is a fundamental aspect of Android development, providing a simple and efficient way to perform background tasks such as network operations, file I/O, or database queries without blocking the main UI thread. AsyncTask is a class provided by the Android framework that allows developers to execute asynchronous operations on a separate worker thread and update the UI thread with the results. One common scenario where AsyncTask is used is fetching data from a remote server or API in response to user interaction, such as loading a list of items from a web service when a user opens a screen or clicks a button. To implement AsyncTask, developers typically create a subclass of AsyncTask and override the doInBackground() method to perform the background task, such as fetching data from a server or performing a long-running computation.

javaCopy code

```
private class MyAsyncTask extends AsyncTask<Void, Void, String> { @Override protected String doInBackground(Void... voids) { // Perform background task, such as fetching data from a server return fetchDataFromServer(); } @Override protected void onPostExecute(String result) { // Update UI with the result of the background task textView.setText(result); } }
```

In this example, the doInBackground() method is responsible for performing the background task, such as fetching data from a server, while the onPostExecute() method is called on the UI thread after the background task is complete, allowing developers to update the UI with the result of the background task. AsyncTask provides three generic types: Params, Progress, and Result. Params represents the input parameters passed to the doInBackground() method, Progress represents the progress of the background task, and Result represents the result returned by the doInBackground() method and passed to the onPostExecute() method.

Additionally, AsyncTask provides methods for reporting progress updates and handling task cancellation. Developers can call the publishProgress() method from within the doInBackground() method to publish progress updates to the UI thread, allowing developers to update UI elements such as progress bars or text views to reflect the progress of the background task. AsyncTask also provides an onProgressUpdate() method that is called on the UI thread whenever a progress update is published, allowing developers to update the UI with the progress of the background task.

javaCopy code

```
private class MyAsyncTask extends AsyncTask<Void, Integer, String> { @Override protected String doInBackground(Void... voids) { // Perform background task, such as fetching data from a server int progress = 0; while (progress < 100) { // Simulate background task progress progress += 10; publishProgress(progress); try { Thread.sleep(1000); } catch (InterruptedException e) { e.printStackTrace(); } } return "Task completed"; } @Override protected void onProgressUpdate(Integer... values) { // Update UI with progress updates progressBar.setProgress(values[0]); } @Override protected
```

```
void onPostExecute(String result) { // Update UI with the result of the background task textView.setText(result); } }
```

In this example, the doInBackground() method simulates a long-running task by incrementing a progress variable and publishing progress updates every second using the publishProgress() method. The onProgressUpdate() method updates the UI with the progress updates, allowing developers to display the progress of the background task to the user. Finally, the onPostExecute() method updates the UI with the result of the background task once it is complete.

AsyncTask also provides methods for handling task cancellation, such as cancel() and isCancelled(). Developers can call the cancel() method to cancel the execution of an AsyncTask, and the isCancelled() method to check if the task has been cancelled. Task cancellation is useful for scenarios where the user navigates away from the screen or cancels an ongoing operation, allowing developers to stop the background task and clean up any resources associated with it.

javaCopy code

```
private class MyAsyncTask extends AsyncTask<Void, Void, String> { @Override protected String doInBackground(Void... voids) { // Check if the task has been cancelled before performing the background task if (isCancelled()) { return null; } // Perform background task, such as fetching data from a server return fetchDataFromServer(); } @Override protected void onPostExecute(String result) { // Update UI with the result of the background task if (result != null) { textView.setText(result); } else { textView.setText("Task cancelled"); } } }
```

In this example, the doInBackground() method checks if the task has been cancelled before performing the background task, and returns null if the task has been cancelled. The onPostExecute() method updates the UI with the result of the background task or a message indicating that the task was cancelled.

In addition to the basic implementation of AsyncTask described above, developers should also be aware of best practices and considerations when using AsyncTask in Android applications. For example, AsyncTask should be used for short-running background tasks that are expected to complete relatively quickly, such as network operations or database queries. Long-running tasks should be executed using other mechanisms such as ThreadPoolExecutor or IntentService to avoid potential memory leaks or performance issues. Additionally, developers should be mindful of the lifecycle of AsyncTask instances and ensure that they are properly managed to avoid issues such as memory leaks or IllegalStateExceptions. Finally, developers should consider using modern alternatives to AsyncTask such as Kotlin coroutines or RxJava, which offer more powerful and flexible APIs for handling asynchronous operations in Android applications.

Overall, AsyncTask is a powerful and versatile class provided by the Android framework for performing background tasks in Android applications. By understanding how to properly implement and use AsyncTask, developers can create responsive and efficient applications that provide a seamless user experience.

Using AsyncTaskLoader for Efficient Data Loading is a crucial aspect of Android app development, especially when dealing with data retrieval from sources such as databases, content providers, or network requests. AsyncTaskLoader is a class provided by the Android framework that extends AsyncTask to load data asynchronously in a way that is more efficient and resilient to configuration changes compared to AsyncTask. AsyncTaskLoader is particularly useful for loading data that needs to be retained across configuration changes, such as screen rotations or changes in device orientation, as it automatically handles the management of the loader's lifecycle and ensures that data is loaded only once and retained across configuration changes. One common scenario where AsyncTaskLoader is used is loading data from a database or content provider in response to user interaction, such as displaying a list of items from a database when a user opens a screen or scrolls through a list.

To implement AsyncTaskLoader, developers typically create a subclass of AsyncTaskLoader and override the loadInBackground() method to perform the background data loading task, such as querying a database or making a network request. AsyncTaskLoader provides built-in support for managing the loader's lifecycle and ensuring that data is loaded only once and retained across configuration changes, making it a convenient and efficient choice for loading data in Android applications.

javaCopy code

```
public class MyDataLoader extends AsyncTaskLoader<List<MyData>> { public MyDataLoader(Context context) { super(context); } @Override public List<MyData> loadInBackground() { // Perform background data loading task, such as querying a database return fetchDataFromDatabase(); } @Override protected void onStartLoading() { forceLoad(); // Force loading of data } }
```

In this example, the loadInBackground() method performs the background data loading task, such as querying a database for a list of items, while the onStartLoading() method is called when the loader is started and initiates the loading of data by calling the forceLoad() method. The AsyncTaskLoader automatically handles the management of the loader's lifecycle and ensures that data is loaded only once and retained across configuration changes, providing a seamless and efficient user experience.

Additionally, AsyncTaskLoader provides methods for monitoring the status of the loader and accessing the loaded data. Developers can register a LoaderCallbacks callback interface to receive notifications when the loader's data is loaded or when the loader's status changes, allowing them to update the UI with the loaded data or display loading indicators to the user. For example, the following code registers a LoaderCallbacks interface to receive notifications when the loader's data is loaded:

javaCopy code

```
getSupportLoaderManager().initLoader(LOADER_ID, null,
new LoaderManager.LoaderCallbacks<List<MyData>>() {
@Override public Loader<List<MyData>>
onCreateLoader(int id, Bundle args) { return new
MyDataLoader(MainActivity.this); } @Override public void
onLoadFinished(Loader<List<MyData>> loader,
List<MyData> data) { // Update UI with loaded data
mAdapter.setData(data); } @Override public void
onLoaderReset(Loader<List<MyData>> loader) { // Clear UI
or reset state mAdapter.setData(null); } });
```

In this example, the initLoader() method is called to initialize the loader with a unique loader ID, the LoaderCallbacks interface is implemented to handle loader callbacks, and the onLoadFinished() method is called when the loader's data is loaded, allowing developers to update the UI with the loaded data.

Moreover, AsyncTaskLoader provides built-in support for cancellation and reloading of data. Developers can call the cancelLoad() method to cancel the loading of data if it is no longer needed, such as when the user navigates away from the screen or cancels an ongoing operation. Additionally, developers can call the restartLoader() method to force the loader to reload its data, such as when the underlying data source has changed and needs to be reloaded. AsyncTaskLoader automatically handles the cancellation and reloading of data, ensuring that data is loaded efficiently and reliably.

javaCopy code

```
@Override protected void onStop() { getSupportLoaderManager().destroyLoader(LOADER_ID); // Destroy loader when activity is stopped super.onStop(); }
```

In this example, the destroyLoader() method is called to destroy the loader when the activity is stopped, preventing any pending background tasks from continuing and releasing any associated resources.

In addition to the basic implementation of AsyncTaskLoader described above, developers should also be aware of best practices and considerations when using AsyncTaskLoader in Android applications. For example, AsyncTaskLoader should be used for loading data that needs to be retained across configuration changes and is expected to be relatively short-lived, such as loading data from a database or content provider. Long-lived tasks or tasks that need to continue running even when the associated activity or fragment is destroyed should be executed using other mechanisms such as foreground services or JobScheduler. Additionally, developers should be mindful of potential memory leaks when using AsyncTaskLoader and ensure that they properly clean up any resources associated with the loader when it is no longer needed.

Overall, AsyncTaskLoader is a powerful and efficient class provided by the Android framework for loading data asynchronously in Android applications. By understanding how to properly implement and use AsyncTaskLoader, developers can create responsive and efficient applications that provide a seamless user experience, even in the face of configuration changes or other interruptions.

Chapter 5: Networking and RESTful APIs Integration

Networking Fundamentals are essential concepts that form the backbone of modern communication systems, enabling devices to exchange data and information across various networks. In the digital age, where connectivity is paramount, understanding networking fundamentals is crucial for developers, system administrators, and anyone involved in building or maintaining computer systems. At its core, networking involves the interconnection of devices, such as computers, servers, smartphones, and IoT devices, to enable communication and data exchange. One fundamental aspect of networking is understanding the concept of network protocols, which are sets of rules and conventions that govern how data is transmitted and received between devices on a network. Protocols define standards for addressing, routing, error detection and correction, and data formatting, allowing devices from different manufacturers and running different operating systems to communicate effectively.

The most widely used networking protocol suite is the TCP/IP (Transmission Control Protocol/Internet Protocol) suite, which forms the basis of the Internet and many other networks. TCP/IP consists of a suite of protocols, including TCP, IP, UDP (User Datagram Protocol), ICMP (Internet Control Message Protocol), and others, each serving a specific purpose in the networking stack. TCP provides reliable, connection-oriented communication between devices, ensuring that data is transmitted in the correct order and is delivered without errors. UDP, on the other hand, is a connectionless, unreliable protocol that is often used for streaming media, real-time communication, and other applications where speed is more important than reliability.

Another fundamental concept in networking is understanding the OSI (Open Systems Interconnection) model, which is a conceptual framework that defines the layers of protocols and services that make up a network. The OSI model consists of seven layers, each responsible for specific functions in the communication process. These layers include the Physical layer, Data Link layer, Network layer, Transport layer, Session layer, Presentation layer, and Application layer. Each layer encapsulates and adds functionality to the data as it traverses the network, providing a modular and standardized approach to networking.

Networking also involves understanding IP addressing and routing, which are fundamental concepts for ensuring that data is routed correctly between devices on a network. IP addressing involves assigning unique numerical identifiers, known as IP addresses, to devices on a network, allowing them to be uniquely identified and addressed. IP addresses are typically divided into two types: IPv4 (Internet Protocol version 4) addresses, which are 32-bit numerical addresses expressed in dotted-decimal notation (e.g., 192.168.1.1), and IPv6 (Internet Protocol version 6) addresses, which are 128-bit numerical addresses expressed in hexadecimal notation (e.g., 2001:0db8:85a3:0000:0000:8a2e:0370:7334). Routing, on the other hand, involves the process of forwarding data packets between devices on different networks based on their destination IP addresses. Routers are devices that perform routing functions, determining the optimal path for data to travel through the network based on routing tables and algorithms.

In addition to IP addressing and routing, networking also involves understanding the Domain Name System (DNS), which is a hierarchical naming system used to translate human-readable domain names (e.g., www.example.com) into IP addresses. DNS servers maintain databases of domain names and their corresponding IP addresses, allowing users to access websites and other resources on the Internet using easy-to-remember domain names instead of numerical IP addresses. DNS resolution is a crucial aspect of Internet communication, enabling devices to locate and connect to servers and services using domain names.

Furthermore, networking encompasses various technologies and protocols for securing communication and data exchange over networks. One fundamental aspect of network security is encryption, which involves encoding data in such a way that only authorized parties can decipher it. Secure communication protocols such as HTTPS (Hypertext Transfer Protocol Secure) use encryption algorithms such as SSL/TLS (Secure Sockets Layer/Transport Layer Security) to encrypt data transmitted between clients and servers, ensuring that sensitive information such as passwords, credit card numbers, and personal data remains confidential and secure. Additionally, firewalls, intrusion detection systems (IDS), and virtual private networks (VPN) are examples of network security technologies used to protect networks from unauthorized access, malware, and other security threats.

Moreover, networking involves understanding the concept of network topologies, which define the physical or logical layout of devices on a network and how they are interconnected. Common network topologies include star, bus, ring, mesh, and hybrid topologies, each with its own advantages and disadvantages in terms of scalability, fault tolerance, and cost. Network administrators must carefully design and configure network topologies to meet the specific requirements of their organization, taking into account factors such as network size, bandwidth requirements, latency, and reliability.

From a practical standpoint, configuring and managing networks often involves using command-line interface (CLI) commands or graphical user interface (GUI) tools provided by networking equipment vendors or operating systems. For example, configuring network interfaces, setting IP addresses, and modifying routing tables on Linux-based systems can be done using CLI tools such as ifconfig, ip, and route, while network troubleshooting and monitoring can be performed using tools such as ping, traceroute, and netstat. Similarly, network configuration and management on Cisco networking devices often involve using CLI commands in the Cisco IOS (Internetwork Operating System) or GUI tools such as Cisco Network Assistant or Cisco Configuration Professional.

In summary, Networking Fundamentals are essential concepts that form the foundation of modern communication systems, enabling devices to exchange data and information across various networks effectively. From understanding network protocols, IP addressing, and routing to mastering network security, DNS, and network topologies, a solid grasp of networking fundamentals is crucial for building and maintaining reliable, secure, and efficient computer networks. Whether you're a developer, system administrator, or IT professional, having a thorough understanding of networking fundamentals is essential for success in today's interconnected world.

RESTful API Integration in Android is a fundamental aspect of mobile app development, enabling Android applications to interact with remote servers and retrieve data using the Representational State Transfer (REST) architectural style. RESTful APIs provide a standardized way for clients, such as Android apps, to communicate with servers over the Hypertext Transfer Protocol (HTTP), using simple and stateless operations such as GET, POST, PUT, DELETE, and PATCH to perform CRUD (Create, Read, Update, Delete) operations on resources. Integrating RESTful APIs into Android apps allows developers to fetch data from external sources, such as web services, databases, or cloud platforms, and display it in the app's user interface, enabling dynamic and real-time content delivery. One common scenario where RESTful API integration is used in Android apps is fetching data from a web service, such as retrieving a list of products from an e-commerce website or fetching user information from a social media platform. To integrate a RESTful API into an Android app, developers typically use HTTP client libraries such as Retrofit, Volley, OkHttp, or AsyncTask to make HTTP requests to the API endpoints and retrieve data in JSON or XML format. Retrofit, in particular, is a popular choice for RESTful API integration in Android due to its simplicity, ease of use, and powerful features for defining API interfaces and handling network requests asynchronously. To use

Retrofit, developers need to define a Java interface that represents the RESTful API endpoints and methods for performing CRUD operations on resources, annotated with Retrofit annotations such as @GET, @POST, @PUT, @DELETE, and @PATCH.

javaCopy code

```
public interface ApiService { @GET("products") Call<List<Product>> getProducts(); @POST("products") Call<Product> createProduct(@Body Product product); @PUT("products/{id}") Call<Product> updateProduct(@Path("id") int productId, @Body Product product); @DELETE("products/{id}") Call<Void> deleteProduct(@Path("id") int productId); }
```

In this example, the ApiService interface defines methods for performing CRUD operations on products, such as retrieving a list of products, creating a new product, updating an existing product, and deleting a product. Retrofit annotations such as @GET, @POST, @PUT, and @DELETE are used to specify the HTTP request method and the relative URL of the API endpoint.

Additionally, developers need to create a Retrofit instance and configure it with a base URL for the API endpoints, as well as any required HTTP client settings such as timeouts, interceptors, or authentication mechanisms. Once configured, developers can use the Retrofit instance to create API service instances and make HTTP requests to the API endpoints asynchronously, handling the response data using callback interfaces or RxJava observables.

javaCopy code

```
Retrofit retrofit = new Retrofit.Builder()
.baseUrl("https://api.example.com/")
```

```
.addConverterFactory(GsonConverterFactory.create())
.build(); ApiService apiService = retrofit.create(ApiService.class); Call<List<Product>> call = apiService.getProducts(); call.enqueue( new Callback<List<Product>>() { @Override public void onResponse(Call<List<Product>> call, Response<List<Product>> response) { if (response.isSuccessful()) { List<Product> products = response.body(); // Process the list of products } else { // Handle error response } } @Override public void onFailure(Call<List<Product>> call, Throwable t) { // Handle network error } });
```

In this example, a Retrofit instance is created with a base URL of "https://api.example.com/" and a GsonConverterFactory for converting JSON responses to Java objects using Gson. An ApiService instance is then created using the Retrofit instance, and an asynchronous HTTP GET request is made to the "products" endpoint using the getProducts() method. The response data is handled in the onResponse() method, where developers can extract the list of products from the response body if the request is successful, or handle error responses or network errors in the onFailure() method.

Furthermore, Retrofit provides support for authentication mechanisms such as OAuth, basic authentication, or token-based authentication, allowing developers to authenticate users and secure access to protected resources on the server. Authentication headers can be added to Retrofit requests using interceptors or custom authentication mechanisms provided by Retrofit's authentication modules. For example, to add a bearer token authentication header to Retrofit requests, developers can create an OkHttpClient instance with an authentication interceptor and configure it with the bearer token obtained from the authentication server.

javaCopy code

```
OkHttpClient.Builder httpClientBuilder = new
OkHttpClient.Builder();
httpClientBuilder.addInterceptor(new Interceptor() {
@Override public Response intercept(Chain chain)
throws IOException { Request originalRequest =
chain.request(); Request.Builder requestBuilder =
originalRequest.newBuilder() .header("Authorization",
"Bearer " + authToken); Request newRequest =
requestBuilder.build(); return
chain.proceed(newRequest); } }); Retrofit retrofit = new
Retrofit.Builder() .baseUrl("https://api.example.com/")
.client(httpClientBuilder.build())
.addConverterFactory(GsonConverterFactory.create())
.build(); ApiService apiService =
retrofit.create(ApiService.class);
```

In this example, an OkHttpClient instance is created with an authentication interceptor that adds a bearer token authentication header to HTTP requests. The OkHttpClient instance is then used to create a Retrofit instance, which is configured with the base URL and GsonConverterFactory as before.

In addition to Retrofit, other HTTP client libraries such as Volley and OkHttp can also be used for RESTful API integration in Android apps. Volley is a fast and efficient HTTP library provided by Google for making network requests in Android apps, offering features such as request prioritization, request cancellation, and automatic request retries. OkHttp is a powerful HTTP client library for Android and Java applications, offering features such as connection pooling, response caching, and transparent gzip compression. Developers can choose the HTTP client library that best fits their requirements and preferences for RESTful API integration in Android apps.

In summary, RESTful API Integration in Android is a fundamental aspect of mobile app development, enabling Android applications to interact with remote servers and retrieve data using the REST architectural style. By using HTTP client libraries such as Retrofit, Volley, or OkHttp, developers can make HTTP requests to API endpoints, handle response data asynchronously, and integrate remote data sources seamlessly into their Android apps. Whether fetching data from web services, databases, or cloud platforms, integrating RESTful APIs allows Android apps to provide dynamic and real-time content, enhancing the user experience and functionality of the app.

Chapter 6: Security Best Practices: Authentication and Authorization

Authentication Methods Overview is crucial for understanding how users prove their identity to gain access to resources or services in computer systems and networks. In today's digital landscape, where security is paramount, implementing robust authentication methods is essential for protecting sensitive information and preventing unauthorized access. Authentication methods come in various forms, ranging from traditional password-based authentication to more advanced techniques such as biometric authentication, multi-factor authentication (MFA), and single sign-on (SSO). Each authentication method has its strengths and weaknesses, and the choice of authentication method depends on factors such as security requirements, user experience, and the specific use case.

One of the most common authentication methods is password-based authentication, where users provide a username and password to authenticate themselves. In this method, users are required to memorize a secret password, which they present along with their username to gain access to a system or service. Passwords are typically stored in hashed or encrypted form in a database to protect them from unauthorized access. To implement password-based authentication, developers can use authentication frameworks and libraries provided by programming languages and frameworks, such as Passport.js for Node.js or Spring Security for Java. Additionally, developers should follow best practices for password security, such as enforcing strong password policies, implementing password hashing algorithms, and protecting against common attacks such as brute force attacks and password guessing.

bashCopy code

```
# Example command to set up password-based authentication in Node.js using Passport.js npm install passport passport-local
```

Another common authentication method is biometric authentication, which uses unique physical characteristics or behavioral traits of an individual, such as fingerprints, facial features, or voice patterns, to verify their identity. Biometric authentication offers a convenient and secure way for users to authenticate themselves without the need for passwords or PINs. Biometric authentication is widely used in mobile devices, laptops, and other electronic devices with built-in biometric sensors. To implement biometric authentication in Android apps, developers can use the BiometricPrompt API provided by the Android framework, which provides a standardized way to integrate biometric authentication into apps across different Android devices.

bashCopy code

```
# Example command to add biometric authentication support to an Android app using BiometricPrompt API implementation 'androidx.biometric:biometric:1.2.0-alpha03'
```

Multi-factor authentication (MFA) is another authentication method that combines two or more authentication factors to verify the identity of a user. MFA enhances security by requiring users to provide multiple pieces of evidence, such as something they know (password), something they have (smartphone or security token), or something they are (biometric trait), to gain access to a system or service. Common MFA methods include one-time passwords (OTP), SMS or email verification codes, hardware tokens, and biometric authentication combined with a PIN or password. Implementing MFA typically involves integrating authentication APIs or services provided by identity providers or authentication platforms, such as Auth0, Okta, or Firebase Authentication.

bashCopy code

```
# Example command to add MFA support to a web application using Auth0 npm install @auth0/auth0-spa-js
```

Single sign-on (SSO) is a centralized authentication mechanism that allows users to authenticate once and access multiple related but independent software systems or services without needing to log in again. SSO enables seamless access to various applications and services within an organization or across different organizations, improving user experience and productivity. Common SSO protocols and standards include OAuth 2.0, OpenID Connect, SAML (Security Assertion Markup Language), and LDAP (Lightweight Directory Access Protocol). Implementing SSO typically involves configuring identity providers, such as Azure Active Directory, Google Identity Platform, or Keycloak, and integrating SSO libraries or SDKs into applications or services.

bashCopy code

```
# Example command to add OAuth 2.0 support to a web application using Auth0 npm install express-openid-connect
```

In addition to these authentication methods, there are other emerging authentication techniques and standards, such as passwordless authentication, WebAuthn (Web Authentication), and FIDO2 (Fast Identity Online 2), which aim to improve security and usability by eliminating passwords altogether or by introducing stronger cryptographic authentication mechanisms. Passwordless authentication methods include email or SMS magic links,

QR code authentication, and authentication through social media accounts. WebAuthn and FIDO2 enable authentication using public key cryptography and authenticators such as security keys, biometric sensors, or built-in authenticators in devices, providing stronger security guarantees and protection against phishing attacks.
Overall, understanding the various authentication methods and their capabilities is essential for designing secure and user-friendly authentication systems in modern computer systems and networks. By choosing the appropriate authentication methods and implementing them correctly, developers can ensure that their applications and services are protected against unauthorized access and provide a seamless and frictionless authentication experience for users. Whether implementing password-based authentication, biometric authentication, MFA, SSO, or emerging authentication techniques, developers should prioritize security, usability, and compliance with relevant regulations and standards to build trust and confidence among users.

Implementing Authorization Mechanisms is a critical aspect of designing secure and controlled access to resources in software systems and applications. Authorization determines what actions users or entities are allowed to perform on specific resources based on their identities and roles. Unlike authentication, which verifies the identity of users, authorization focuses on determining the permissions and privileges granted to authenticated users or entities. Effective authorization mechanisms help protect sensitive information, prevent unauthorized access, and enforce compliance with security policies and regulations. There are various authorization mechanisms and techniques available, each with its strengths, weaknesses, and use cases.

One common authorization mechanism is Role-Based Access Control (RBAC), which is based on the concept of assigning roles to users and granting permissions to those roles. In RBAC, users are assigned one or more roles based on their job responsibilities or functions within an organization, and permissions are granted to roles rather than individual users. This simplifies administration and management by centralizing permissions at the role level and reduces the complexity of managing access control lists for individual users. To implement RBAC, developers typically define roles, permissions, and role-permission mappings in a centralized access control system or database and enforce access control checks based on the user's assigned roles.

bashCopy code

```
# Example command to install RBAC library in a Node.js application using npm npm install rbac
```

Attribute-Based Access Control (ABAC) is another authorization mechanism that relies on attributes or characteristics of users, resources, and the environment to make access control decisions. ABAC evaluates access requests based on a set of attributes such as user attributes (e.g., role, department, location), resource attributes (e.g., sensitivity, type), and environmental attributes (e.g., time, location), and dynamically determines whether to grant or deny access based on predefined policies or rules. ABAC provides fine-grained access control and flexibility to adapt access policies based on changing conditions, making it suitable for complex and dynamic environments such as cloud computing and IoT (Internet of Things) ecosystems.

bashCopy code

```
# Example command to install ABAC library in a Python application using pip pip install py-abac
```

Another authorization mechanism is Attribute-Based Access Control (ABAC), which relies on attributes or characteristics of users, resources, and the environment to make access control decisions. ABAC evaluates access requests based on a set of attributes such as user attributes (e.g., role, department, location), resource attributes (e.g., sensitivity, type), and environmental attributes (e.g., time, location), and dynamically determines whether to grant or deny access based on predefined policies or rules. ABAC provides fine-grained access control and flexibility to adapt access policies based on changing conditions, making it suitable for complex and dynamic environments such as cloud computing and IoT (Internet of Things) ecosystems.

bashCopy code

```
# Example command to install ABAC library in a Python application using pip pip install py-abac
```

OAuth 2.0 is a widely used authorization framework that enables delegated access to resources on behalf of users without sharing their credentials. OAuth 2.0 is commonly used in web and mobile applications to allow users to grant limited access to their protected resources, such as social media profiles or cloud storage, to third-party applications or services. OAuth 2.0 defines roles such as resource owner, client, authorization server, and resource server, and uses authorization grants such as authorization code, implicit, client credentials, and refresh token to facilitate secure authorization and access delegation. To implement OAuth 2.0 in applications, developers can use OAuth 2.0 libraries and SDKs provided by identity providers or authentication platforms, such as Auth0, Okta, or Firebase Authentication.

bashCopy code

```
# Example command to add OAuth 2.0 support to a web application using Auth0 npm install express-openid-connect
```

JSON Web Tokens (JWT) is a popular standard for representing claims securely between two parties, such as an identity provider and a service provider, using JSON-based tokens. JWT enables stateless authentication and authorization by encoding user claims and signing them with a digital signature to ensure their integrity and authenticity. JWT tokens are typically used in token-based authentication and authorization mechanisms such as OAuth 2.0 and OpenID Connect, where tokens are issued by an authorization server and presented by clients to access protected resources. To implement JWT-based authorization in applications, developers can use JWT libraries and middleware provided by programming languages and frameworks, such as jsonwebtoken for Node.js or PyJWT for Python.

bashCopy code

```
# Example command to install JWT library in a Node.js application using npm npm install jsonwebtoken
```

In addition to these authorization mechanisms, there are other emerging techniques and standards for authorization, such as Attribute-Based Access Control (ABAC), Policy-Based Access Control (PBAC), and Externalized Authorization Management (EAM), which aim to provide more dynamic, flexible, and adaptive access control solutions. ABAC extends RBAC by considering attributes of users, resources, and the environment in access control decisions, PBAC defines access control policies based on rules or conditions, and EAM separates authorization logic from application code and externalizes it to a centralized authorization server or policy decision point. These advanced authorization techniques offer greater control, granularity, and scalability in managing access to resources in complex and dynamic environments.

Overall, implementing effective authorization mechanisms is essential for protecting sensitive information, enforcing access control policies, and ensuring compliance with security requirements and regulations in software systems and applications. By choosing the appropriate authorization mechanism based on the specific use case, security requirements, and organizational needs, developers can build secure, scalable, and compliant systems that protect against unauthorized access and mitigate security risks. Whether using RBAC, ABAC, OAuth 2.0, JWT, or other authorization techniques, developers should prioritize security, usability, and maintainability to achieve robust and reliable access control solutions.

Chapter 7: Leveraging Location and Maps Services

Location Awareness in Android is a pivotal feature that empowers developers to create location-based applications, enabling users to interact with content and services tailored to their geographical context. Leveraging the device's GPS, Wi-Fi, cellular network, and other location sensors, Android apps can determine the user's current location, track their movements, and provide location-based functionalities such as mapping, navigation, geofencing, and location-based notifications. Implementing location awareness in Android apps involves integrating location APIs provided by the Android framework, utilizing location permissions, and handling location updates efficiently to deliver accurate and reliable location-based experiences.

The Android framework provides several APIs and classes for accessing location information, the most prominent being the LocationManager and FusedLocationProviderClient. The LocationManager class enables developers to retrieve location updates from various location providers, including GPS, network, and passive providers. Developers can use the LocationManager to request location updates, specify the desired accuracy, update frequency, and criteria for selecting the best location provider based on the device's current state and accuracy requirements.

bashCopy code

```
# Example command to request location updates using LocationManager in Android
```

```
locationManager.requestLocationUpdates(LocationManager.GPS_PROVIDER, 1000, 10, locationListener);
```

The FusedLocationProviderClient is a higher-level location API introduced in the Google Play services library, which offers a more efficient and battery-friendly way to retrieve location updates by intelligently selecting the best location provider based on the device's hardware capabilities, power consumption, and accuracy requirements. The FusedLocationProviderClient abstracts away the complexities of managing location providers and provides a simplified interface for requesting location updates and retrieving the user's last known location.

bashCopy code

```
# Example command to request location updates using FusedLocationProviderClient in Android fusedLocationProviderClient.requestLocationUpdates(locationRequest, locationCallback, Looper.getMainLooper());
```

Before accessing location information in Android apps, developers must request permission from the user to access their device's location. Starting from Android 6.0 (API level 23), Android introduced a runtime permission system that requires apps to request permission from the user at runtime for accessing sensitive features such as location, camera, and contacts. Developers can request location permissions using the ActivityCompat.requestPermissions() method and handle the user's response using the onRequestPermissionsResult() callback method.

javaCopy code

```
// Example code to request location permissions in an Android activity String[] permissions =
```

```
{Manifest.permission.ACCESS_FINE_LOCATION,
Manifest.permission.ACCESS_COARSE_LOCATION};        if
(ContextCompat.checkSelfPermission(this,
Manifest.permission.ACCESS_FINE_LOCATION)          !=
PackageManager.PERMISSION_GRANTED)                  {
ActivityCompat.requestPermissions(this,    permissions,
REQUEST_LOCATION_PERMISSION); }
```

To provide a seamless and user-friendly location-based experience, Android apps should handle location updates efficiently to minimize battery drain and optimize resource usage. This involves implementing strategies such as requesting location updates only when necessary, adjusting the update frequency and accuracy based on the app's requirements, and optimizing location updates using techniques such as batching, geofencing, and activity recognition.

Geofencing is a location-based service that allows developers to define virtual boundaries or geofences around specific geographic areas and trigger notifications or actions when the device enters or exits these geofences. Android provides the Geofencing API, which enables developers to create and manage geofences, monitor the device's proximity to geofences, and receive geofence transition events. Geofencing is commonly used in location-based marketing, location-based reminders, and location-based authentication to provide context-aware experiences to users.

javaCopy code

```
// Example code to create a geofence using the
GeofencingClient in Android Geofence geofence = new
Geofence.Builder()          .setRequestId("myGeofence")
```

```
.setCircularRegion(latitude, longitude, radius) .setExpirationDuration(Geofence.NEVER_EXPIRE) .setTransitionTypes(Geofence.GEOFENCE_TRANSITION_ENTER | Geofence.GEOFENCE_TRANSITION_EXIT) .build(); GeofencingRequest request = new GeofencingRequest.Builder() .addGeofence(geofence) .setInitialTrigger(GeofencingRequest.INITIAL_TRIGGER_ENTER) .build(); geofencingClient.addGeofences(request, pendingIntent);
```

In addition to geofencing, Android apps can utilize other location-based features such as mapping and navigation by integrating mapping libraries and APIs such as Google Maps Android API, Mapbox Android SDK, or OpenStreetMap. These mapping libraries provide powerful features for displaying maps, adding markers, overlays, and polylines, and performing advanced operations such as routing, geocoding, and reverse geocoding.

bashCopy code

```
# Example command to add Google Maps Android API to an Android app using Gradle implementation 'com.google.android.gms:play-services-maps:17.0.0'
```

Location awareness in Android apps opens up a myriad of possibilities for creating innovative and context-aware applications that leverage the user's geographical context to deliver personalized and relevant experiences. Whether it's providing location-based recommendations, tracking fitness activities, or enhancing social networking features, location awareness empowers developers to create immersive and engaging user experiences that resonate with users' real-world interactions and preferences. By leveraging the Android location APIs, handling location permissions effectively, and implementing best practices for location updates and battery optimization, developers can build robust and user-friendly location-based applications that delight users and add value to their lives.

Integrating Maps Services into Your App is a pivotal aspect of modern app development, enabling developers to incorporate interactive maps, location-based services, and geospatial functionalities into their applications. Maps services provide users with visual representations of geographic data, allowing them to explore and interact with maps, search for places, get directions, and discover nearby points of interest. Whether it's building navigation apps, delivery tracking systems, or location-based gaming applications, integrating maps services can greatly enhance the user experience and add value to your app. Several mapping platforms and APIs are available for developers to integrate maps services into their apps, with Google Maps Platform, Mapbox, and OpenStreetMap being some of the most popular choices.

The Google Maps Platform offers a comprehensive set of APIs and SDKs for integrating maps, location-based services, and geospatial data into Android, iOS, and web applications. To integrate Google Maps into your Android app, you first need to enable the Maps SDK for Android and obtain an API key from the Google Cloud Console. Once you have obtained the API key, you can add the Google Maps Android API dependency to your app's build.gradle file and initialize the map in your activity or fragment layout XML file.

bashCopy code

```
# Example command to enable Maps SDK for Android and obtain an API key # Replace YOUR_API_KEY with your actual API key gcloud services enable maps-android-backend.googleapis.com gcloud services enable maps-android-backend.googleapis.com gcloud services enable maps-android-backend.googleapis.com
```

xmlCopy code

```
<!-- Example code to add Google Maps view to an Android layout XML file --> <fragment android:id="@+id/map_fragment" android:name="com.google.android.gms.maps.SupportMapFragment" android:layout_width="match_parent" android:layout_height="match_parent" />
```

In addition to displaying maps, the Google Maps Android API provides features such as marker placement, polyline drawing, heatmaps, and street view, allowing developers to create rich and interactive map-based experiences. Developers can customize the map appearance, add markers to indicate specific locations, draw polylines to represent routes or boundaries, and overlay heatmaps to visualize data density or distribution on the map.

javaCopy code

```
// Example code to add a marker to a Google Map in an Android activity GoogleMap map = ((SupportMapFragment) getSupportFragmentManager().findFragmentById(R.id.map_fragment)).getMap(); LatLng location = new LatLng(37.7749, -122.4194); map.addMarker(new MarkerOptions().position(location).title("Marker Title"));
```

Mapbox is another popular mapping platform that offers a suite of APIs and SDKs for creating custom maps, adding location-based features, and integrating mapping functionalities into mobile and web applications. Mapbox provides highly customizable maps with options to change map styles, add custom markers, overlays, and annotations, and display interactive data layers. To integrate Mapbox into your Android app, you need to sign up for a Mapbox account, create a map style using the Mapbox Studio, and obtain an access token.

bashCopy code

```
# Example command to sign up for a Mapbox account and obtain an access token # Replace YOUR_ACCESS_TOKEN with your actual access token curl "https://api.mapbox.com/styles/v1/mapbox/streets-v11?access_token=YOUR_ACCESS_TOKEN"
```

xmlCopy code

```
<!-- Example code to add Mapbox map view to an Android layout XML file -->
<com.mapbox.mapboxsdk.maps.MapView
android:id="@+id/mapView"
android:layout_width="match_parent"
android:layout_height="match_parent"
mapbox:mapbox_styleUrl="mapbox://styles/mapbox/streets-v11"
mapbox:mapbox_accessToken="YOUR_ACCESS_TOKEN"
/>
```

Once you have obtained the access token, you can add the Mapbox SDK dependency to your app's build.gradle file and initialize the map view in your activity or fragment layout XML file. Mapbox provides a variety of map styles to choose from, including streets, satellite, outdoors, and dark mode, allowing developers to customize the map appearance to suit their app's theme and branding.

javaCopy code

```java
// Example code to add a marker to a Mapbox map in an Android activity mapboxMap.addMarker(new MarkerOptions() .position(new LatLng(37.7749, -122.4194)) .title("Marker Title"));
```

OpenStreetMap (OSM) is an open-source mapping project that provides free and editable map data to the public. Unlike proprietary mapping platforms such as Google Maps and Mapbox, OpenStreetMap allows developers to access, use, and contribute to map data freely without restrictions. To integrate OpenStreetMap into your Android app, you can use third-party libraries such as osmdroid or Mapsforge, which provide APIs for displaying OSM tiles, adding markers, overlays, and annotations, and interacting with map features.

bashCopy code

```bash
# Example command to add osmdroid library to an Android app using Gradle implementation 'org.osmdroid:osmdroid-android:6.1.8'
```

xmlCopy code

```xml
<!-- Example code to add osmdroid MapView to an Android layout XML file -->
<org.osmdroid.views.MapView
android:id="@+id/mapView"
android:layout_width="match_parent"
android:layout_height="match_parent" />
```

In summary, integrating maps services into your app opens up a world of possibilities for creating location-aware and interactive experiences for users. Whether you choose Google Maps Platform, Mapbox, or OpenStreetMap, each mapping platform offers unique features, customization options, and pricing models to suit different app requirements and use cases. By leveraging maps services, developers can enhance the functionality, usability, and engagement of their apps, providing users with valuable location-based information and services that enrich their overall app experience. Whether you're building a travel app, a delivery tracking system, or a location-based game, integrating maps services into your app is essential for delivering compelling and immersive user experiences that keep users coming back for more.

Chapter 8: Advanced Database Management with Room Persistence Library

Introduction to Room Persistence Library is essential for understanding how to effectively manage and persist data in Android applications using a robust and efficient ORM (Object-Relational Mapping) framework. Room is part of the Android Jetpack library and provides an abstraction layer over SQLite, the native relational database engine used in Android. Leveraging Room, developers can easily create, read, update, and delete data from SQLite databases using simple annotations and queries, without the need to write complex SQL statements or manage low-level database operations manually. Room simplifies database operations, improves code readability, and enhances productivity by offering powerful features such as compile-time verification, type-safe queries, and built-in support for LiveData and RxJava.

To integrate Room into an Android project, developers need to add the Room library dependency to the app's build.gradle file and configure the Room database instance in the app's application class or activity.

bashCopy code

```
# Example command to add Room library dependency to an Android app using Gradle implementation "androidx.room:room-runtime:2.4.0"
```

javaCopy code

```
// Example code to configure Room database instance in an Android application class @Database(entities = {User.class}, version = 1) public abstract class AppDatabase extends RoomDatabase { public abstract UserDao userDao();
```

```
private static AppDatabase INSTANCE; public static AppDatabase getInstance(Context context) { if (INSTANCE == null ) { synchronized (AppDatabase.class) { if (INSTANCE == null ) { INSTANCE = Room.databaseBuilder(context.getApplicationContext(), AppDatabase.class, "app_database" ) .build(); } } } return INSTANCE; } }
```

Once Room is integrated into the project, developers can define entity classes to represent database tables and DAO (Data Access Object) interfaces to define database operations such as insert, update, delete, and query. Entity classes in Room are annotated with @Entity to specify the database table schema, while DAO interfaces are annotated with @Dao and contain method declarations for performing database operations.

javaCopy code

```
// Example code to define an entity class in Room @Entity(tableName = "users") public class User { @PrimaryKey public int id; @ColumnInfo(name = "first_name") public String firstName; @ColumnInfo(name = "last_name") public String lastName; } // Example code to define a DAO interface in Room @Dao public interface UserDao { @Insert void insert(User user); @Update void update(User user); @Delete void delete(User user); @Query("SELECT * FROM users") List<User> getAllUsers() ; }
```

Room provides compile-time verification of SQL queries, which means that syntax errors and database schema mismatches are detected during the compilation process rather than at runtime, ensuring greater reliability and stability of the app. Room also offers type-safe queries using Java or Kotlin query methods, allowing developers to write database queries with compile-time type checking and autocompletion support in the IDE.

javaCopy code

```
// Example code to perform database operations using Room AppDatabase db = AppDatabase.getInstance(context); UserDao userDao = db.userDao(); // Insert a new user User user = new User(); user.id = 1; user.firstName = "John"; user.lastName = "Doe"; userDao.insert(user); // Retrieve all users List<User> users = userDao.getAllUsers();
```

Room also provides built-in support for LiveData, a lifecycle-aware observable data holder class, which allows developers to observe changes to database data and update the UI automatically when data changes occur. By using LiveData with Room, developers can create reactive and responsive UIs that reflect real-time changes to database data, providing users with a seamless and immersive experience.

javaCopy code

```
// Example code to observe database changes using LiveData with Room LiveData<List<User>> usersLiveData = userDao.getAllUsersLiveData(); usersLiveData.observe(this, users -> { // Update UI with new list of users });
```

Moreover, Room offers support for RxJava, a popular reactive programming library for composing asynchronous and event-based programs. By integrating Room with RxJava, developers can perform database operations asynchronously, handle errors gracefully, and chain database queries and transformations easily using RxJava's powerful operators.

javaCopy code

```
// Example code to perform database operations asynchronously using RxJava with Room
```

```
userDao.getAllUsersRx()        .subscribeOn(Schedulers.io())
.observeOn(AndroidSchedulers.mainThread())
.subscribe(users -> { // Update UI with new list of users },
throwable -> { // Handle error });
```

In summary, Room Persistence Library is a powerful and efficient ORM framework for managing and persisting data in Android applications. By simplifying database operations, providing compile-time verification of queries, and offering built-in support for LiveData and RxJava, Room simplifies the development of data-driven Android apps and enhances productivity. Whether you're building a simple note-taking app or a complex enterprise application, Room provides the tools and features you need to manage and interact with SQLite databases seamlessly. With its intuitive API and robust capabilities, Room empowers developers to create high-quality Android apps that deliver exceptional user experiences.

Advanced Database Operations with Room is essential for mastering the intricacies of managing and manipulating data in SQLite databases within Android applications. Room, as part of the Android Jetpack library, offers a robust and intuitive framework for performing various database operations efficiently, including complex queries, transactions, migrations, and data manipulation. By delving into advanced database operations with Room, developers can optimize database performance, handle complex data relationships, and implement advanced features such as full-text search, data synchronization, and offline caching. Room simplifies the process of working with databases in Android apps, providing a high-level abstraction layer that abstracts away the complexities of SQLite and offers powerful features for managing database interactions.

One of the advanced database operations supported by Room is the execution of complex queries to retrieve, filter, and aggregate data from database tables. Room allows developers to write SQL queries directly or use Query DSL (Domain Specific Language) provided by Room to construct queries dynamically. Query DSL offers type-safe query construction, compile-time verification, and autocompletion support in the IDE, making it easier to write and maintain complex queries without errors.

javaCopy code

```
// Example code to execute a complex query using Room's Query DSL @Query("SELECT * FROM users WHERE age > :minAge") List<User> getUsersWithMinimumAge(int minAge);
```

Room also supports data manipulation operations such as insert, update, and delete, allowing developers to modify database records efficiently. By annotating DAO methods with @Insert, @Update, and @Delete annotations, developers can define methods for performing these operations and invoke them to add, update, or remove data from database tables.

javaCopy code

```
// Example code to perform data manipulation operations using Room @Insert void insert(User user); @Update void update(User user); @Delete void delete(User user);
```

Transactions are another important aspect of advanced database operations with Room, enabling developers to group multiple database operations into a single atomic unit of work. Transactions ensure data consistency and integrity by guaranteeing that either all operations within the transaction are executed successfully or none of them are. Room supports transactions using the @Transaction annotation, allowing developers to annotate DAO methods with @Transaction to indicate that they should be executed within a transaction.

javaCopy code

```
// Example code to execute database operations within a transaction using Room @Transaction void performTransaction() { // Perform multiple database operations within a single transaction insert(user1); update(user2); delete(user3); }
```

Room also provides support for database migrations, which are necessary when modifying the database schema or migrating data between different database versions. Database migrations allow developers to update the database schema and migrate existing data without losing data integrity or consistency. Room automatically handles database migrations by generating migration scripts based on the differences between the old and new database schemas.

javaCopy code

```
// Example code to define database migrations using Room @Database(version = 2, exportSchema = false) public abstract class AppDatabase extends RoomDatabase { public static final Migration MIGRATION_1_2 = new Migration(1, 2) { @Override public void migrate(@NonNull SupportSQLiteDatabase database) { // Define migration logic to update database schema and migrate data database.execSQL("ALTER TABLE users ADD COLUMN email TEXT"); } }; }
```

Full-text search is another advanced feature supported by Room, allowing developers to perform efficient text-based searches on database tables containing large amounts of textual data. Room provides support for full-text search using the MATCH operator in SQL queries and FTS (Full-Text

Search) tables, which are special virtual tables optimized for full-text search operations.

javaCopy code

```
// Example code to perform full-text search using Room @Query("SELECT * FROM articles WHERE article_text MATCH :query") List<Article> searchArticles(String query);
```

In addition to these advanced database operations, Room offers support for complex data relationships, lazy loading, and database triggers, allowing developers to model and manage complex data structures effectively. Room's support for LiveData and RxJava enables developers to create reactive and responsive apps that reflect real-time changes to database data, providing users with seamless and immersive experiences.

In summary, mastering advanced database operations with Room is essential for building robust and efficient Android applications that effectively manage and manipulate data. By leveraging Room's powerful features for executing complex queries, performing data manipulation operations, handling transactions and migrations, and implementing advanced features such as full-text search and data synchronization, developers can create high-quality apps that deliver exceptional user experiences. With its intuitive API, seamless integration with Android architecture components, and support for modern programming paradigms, Room simplifies the process of working with databases in Android apps and empowers developers to focus on building innovative and impactful features for their apps.

Chapter 9: Implementing MVVM Architecture with Android Architecture Components

MVVM (Model-View-ViewModel) Architecture Overview provides a comprehensive understanding of a design pattern widely employed in modern software development, particularly in building user interfaces for web and mobile applications. MVVM separates the user interface (View) from the business logic (ViewModel) and the data model (Model), fostering better organization, maintainability, and testability of code. In the MVVM pattern, the Model represents the data and business logic of the application, encapsulating data access and manipulation operations. The View is responsible for presenting the user interface to the user and receiving user input, while the ViewModel acts as an intermediary between the View and the Model, handling communication, data binding, and logic related to the presentation layer.

To implement MVVM architecture in an application, developers typically start by defining the data model (Model) to represent the underlying data and business logic. The data model can include classes, structures, or data access objects that encapsulate data retrieval, storage, and manipulation operations. These classes are responsible for interacting with databases, web services, or other data sources to fetch and update data.

bashCopy code

```
# Example command to create a new data model class in a Java project  touch DataModel.java
```

Next, developers design the user interface (View) using layout files, XML files, or UI components specific to the platform. The View is responsible for displaying data to the user, handling user input events, and forwarding user actions to the ViewModel for processing. In Android development, Views are typically implemented using XML layout files for defining UI elements such as buttons, text fields, and images, and Activity or Fragment classes for managing UI interactions.

bashCopy code

```
# Example command to create a new XML layout file for an Android activity touch activity_main.xml
```

After defining the View, developers create the ViewModel, which acts as an intermediary between the View and the Model, providing data to the View and handling user interactions. The ViewModel exposes data and operations relevant to the View using observable properties and commands, allowing the View to observe changes in the data and react accordingly. In Android development, ViewModels are often implemented as separate classes that extend the ViewModel class provided by the Android Architecture Components library.

bashCopy code

```
# Example command to create a new ViewModel class in an Android project touch MainViewModel.java
```

Once the ViewModel is implemented, developers establish communication between the View and the ViewModel using data binding or event-driven mechanisms. Data binding frameworks such as Android Data Binding or libraries like RxJava facilitate two-way data binding between the View and the ViewModel, enabling automatic synchronization of data between the two components. Alternatively, developers can use event-driven approaches such as callbacks or observables to notify the ViewModel of user actions and update the View accordingly.

javaCopy code

```
// Example code to implement two-way data binding in an Android XML layout file <EditText
android:id="@+id/editText"
android:text="@={viewModel.text}"
android:layout_width="wrap_content"
android:layout_height="wrap_content" />
```

javaCopy code

```
// Example code to observe LiveData changes in an Android activity or fragment viewModel.getData().observe(this,
data -> { // Update UI with new data });
```

One of the key benefits of MVVM architecture is its support for unit testing, which allows developers to test individual components of the application in isolation. By separating the business logic (ViewModel) from the user interface (View), developers can write unit tests for the ViewModel without the need for a user interface, making testing faster and more reliable. Unit tests can verify the correctness of data manipulation operations, business logic, and interaction with the Model, ensuring that the application behaves as expected under different scenarios.

bashCopy code

```
# Example command to run unit tests for a ViewModel class in a Java project ./gradlew test
```

Another advantage of MVVM architecture is its support for reusability and maintainability of code. By encapsulating data and presentation logic within the ViewModel, developers can reuse ViewModel components across multiple Views, reducing code duplication and improving code consistency. This also simplifies maintenance and updates, as changes to the business logic can be made in a single location without affecting the user interface or other components of the application.

MVVM architecture promotes separation of concerns and the single responsibility principle, making it easier to understand, modify, and extend the codebase. By organizing code into distinct layers (Model, View, ViewModel), developers can achieve better code structure, readability, and scalability, leading to improved developer productivity and code quality. Moreover, MVVM architecture aligns well with modern software development practices such as modularization, dependency injection, and reactive programming, enabling developers to build robust, flexible, and maintainable applications that meet the evolving needs of users and stakeholders.

In summary, MVVM architecture offers a structured and efficient approach to building modern software applications, providing clear separation of concerns, reusability of code, and support for unit testing. By adopting MVVM architecture, developers can create well-designed, maintainable, and scalable applications that deliver a superior user experience and meet the demands of today's dynamic software market. Whether developing web, mobile, or desktop applications, MVVM architecture provides a solid foundation for building high-quality software solutions that stand the test of time.

Utilizing Android Architecture Components for MVVM is crucial for building robust, scalable, and maintainable Android applications that adhere to modern software design principles. Android Architecture Components, introduced by Google as part of the Android Jetpack library, provide a set of libraries, guidelines, and best practices for structuring Android apps using the Model-View-ViewModel (MVVM) architecture pattern. By leveraging Android Architecture Components, developers can simplify and streamline the development process, improve code quality, and enhance the overall user experience of their apps. The key components of Android Architecture Components include LiveData, ViewModel, Room, and Data Binding, each serving a specific purpose in facilitating the implementation of MVVM architecture in Android apps.

LiveData, one of the core components of Android Architecture Components, is an observable data holder class that is lifecycle-aware, meaning it automatically updates its value based on the lifecycle state of the observing component, typically an Activity or Fragment. LiveData ensures that UI components always display the latest data from the ViewModel, and it automatically unsubscribes observers when their associated lifecycle is destroyed, preventing memory leaks and crashes. LiveData simplifies the implementation of reactive UIs in Android apps, allowing developers to observe changes to data in the ViewModel and update the UI accordingly.

javaCopy code

```
// Example code to create a LiveData object in a ViewModel private MutableLiveData<String> mTextLiveData = new MutableLiveData<>(); // Example code to observe LiveData changes in an Activity or Fragment viewModel.getTextLiveData().observe(this, text -> { // Update UI with new text });
```

ViewModel is another important component of Android Architecture Components, responsible for managing UI-related data and handling communication between the View (UI) and the underlying data model. ViewModels are designed to survive configuration changes such as screen rotations and activity recreation, ensuring that UI data is preserved across device rotations and other lifecycle events. ViewModel instances are typically scoped to the lifecycle of a UI component, such as an Activity or Fragment, and they store UI-related data in a lifecycle-aware manner, allowing UI components to observe changes to the data and update themselves accordingly.

javaCopy code

```
// Example code to create a ViewModel class in an Android app public class MyViewModel extends ViewModel { private MutableLiveData<String> mData = new MutableLiveData<>(); public LiveData<String> getData() { return mData; } public void setData(String data) { mData.setValue(data); } }
```

Room Persistence Library, another component of Android Architecture Components, provides an abstraction layer over SQLite, the native relational database engine used in Android. Room simplifies database operations in Android apps by allowing developers to define database entities, access objects, and database operations using annotations and compile-time checks. Room generates boilerplate code for handling database operations, such as CRUD (Create, Read, Update, Delete) operations and database migrations, making it easier to work with databases in Android apps.

javaCopy code

```
// Example code to define a Room entity class representing a table in the database @Entity(tableName = "users") public class User { @PrimaryKey private int id; @ColumnInfo(name = "name") private String name; // Getters and setters }
```

Data Binding is a feature of Android Architecture Components that allows developers to bind UI components in layout files directly to data sources in the ViewModel, eliminating the need for manual findViewById() calls and reducing boilerplate code. Data Binding facilitates two-way data binding between UI components and data sources, enabling automatic synchronization of data between the View and the ViewModel. Data Binding improves code readability, reduces bugs, and enhances developer productivity by simplifying the process of updating UI components with data from the ViewModel.

xmlCopy code

```
<!-- Example code to use data binding in an Android layout
file --> <layout
xmlns:android="http://schemas.android.com/apk/res/andro
id"> <data> <variable name="viewModel"
type="com.example.MyViewModel" /> </data>
<LinearLayout android:layout_width="match_parent"
android:layout_height="match_parent"
android:orientation="vertical"> <TextView
android:layout_width="wrap_content"
android:layout_height="wrap_content"
android:text="@{viewModel.getData()}" /> </LinearLayout>
</layout>
```

To utilize Android Architecture Components for MVVM in an Android app, developers can follow a step-by-step approach:

Define the data model and database entities using Room annotations.

Implement the ViewModel class to manage UI-related data and business logic.

Create layout files for UI components and use Data Binding to bind UI elements to ViewModel properties.

Use LiveData to observe changes to ViewModel data and update the UI accordingly.

Integrate Room Persistence Library to handle database operations and manage app data.

Test the application thoroughly to ensure that it behaves as expected under different scenarios and device configurations.

By following these steps and leveraging Android Architecture Components, developers can build modern, maintainable, and scalable Android applications that deliver a superior user experience. Android Architecture Components promote best practices in Android app development, including separation of concerns, testability, and lifecycle management, making them an essential tool for Android developers seeking to build high-quality apps.

Chapter 10: Performance Optimization Techniques for High-Quality Apps

Performance profiling tools are indispensable assets for developers striving to optimize the speed, efficiency, and resource consumption of their software applications. These tools offer insights into various aspects of an application's performance, including CPU usage, memory allocation, network activity, and rendering performance, allowing developers to identify bottlenecks, inefficiencies, and areas for improvement. By analyzing performance metrics and profiling application behavior, developers can pinpoint performance issues, prioritize optimization efforts, and ultimately deliver faster, more responsive, and more reliable applications. Performance profiling tools come in various forms, including built-in development tools, third-party libraries, and cloud-based services, each offering unique features and capabilities to meet the diverse needs of developers across different platforms and development environments.

One of the most widely used performance profiling tools for Android development is Android Profiler, a set of integrated performance monitoring tools included in Android Studio. Android Profiler provides real-time insights into key performance metrics such as CPU usage, memory usage, network activity, and UI rendering performance, allowing developers to monitor and analyze their app's performance directly from within the IDE. Android Profiler offers features such as CPU Profiler, Memory Profiler, Network Profiler, and GPU Profiler, each providing detailed insights into specific aspects of an app's performance.

bashCopy code

Example command to open Android Profiler in Android Studio ./studio.sh

Another popular performance profiling tool for Android development is Systrace, a command-line tool that captures system traces of Android devices to analyze system behavior and performance. Systrace provides detailed insights into various system-level events, including CPU scheduling, disk I/O, and graphics rendering, allowing developers to identify performance bottlenecks and optimize system resource usage. Systrace generates trace files in the Chrome Tracing format, which can be analyzed using Chrome's built-in tracing tools or custom analysis tools developed by the developer.

bashCopy code

Example command to capture a system trace using Systrace adb shell systrace.py -o trace.html

For iOS development, Xcode offers a suite of performance profiling tools known as Instruments, which provide insights into various aspects of an iOS app's performance, including CPU usage, memory allocation, energy usage, and network activity. Instruments offers a wide range of profiling templates, including Time Profiler, Allocations, Leaks, and Network, each tailored to specific performance analysis tasks. With Instruments, developers can identify performance issues, memory leaks, and energy inefficiencies in their iOS apps and take appropriate measures to optimize performance and improve user experience.

bashCopy code

Example command to open Instruments in Xcode open /Applications/Xcode.app/Contents/Applications/Instrument s.app

In addition to built-in development tools, developers can also leverage third-party performance profiling libraries and frameworks to analyze and optimize the performance of their applications. For example, LeakCanary is a popular open-source library for Android development that detects and analyzes memory leaks in Android apps, helping developers identify and fix memory-related performance issues. Similarly, Firebase Performance Monitoring is a cloud-based service provided by Google that enables developers to monitor and analyze the performance of their Android and iOS apps in real-time, including network latency, app startup time, and screen rendering performance.

bashCopy code

```
# Example command to integrate LeakCanary library into an Android project using Gradle implementation 'com.squareup.leakcanary:leakcanary-android:2.7'
```

bashCopy code

```
# Example command to integrate Firebase Performance Monitoring into an Android project using Gradle implementation 'com.google.firebase:firebase-performance:20.0.0'
```

In summary, performance profiling tools play a critical role in the development process, enabling developers to identify, analyze, and optimize the performance of their software applications effectively. Whether developing for Android, iOS, or other platforms, developers can leverage a variety of performance profiling tools, including built-in development tools, third-party libraries, and cloud-based services, to gain insights into their app's performance characteristics and improve overall quality. By incorporating performance profiling into the development workflow, developers can ensure that their applications meet performance standards, deliver a superior user experience, and remain competitive in today's fast-paced digital landscape.

Advanced Optimization Strategies are indispensable for developers seeking to squeeze every ounce of performance and efficiency out of their software applications, particularly in resource-constrained environments such as mobile devices, embedded systems, and cloud computing platforms. These strategies encompass a wide range of techniques, algorithms, and best practices aimed at reducing latency, minimizing resource usage, improving scalability, and enhancing the overall performance of applications. By employing advanced optimization strategies, developers can achieve significant performance gains, deliver faster, more responsive, and more reliable applications, and ultimately provide a better user experience to their audience. Advanced optimization strategies span various areas of software development, including algorithm optimization, code optimization, system optimization, and architectural optimization, each addressing specific aspects of performance improvement and efficiency enhancement.

One of the fundamental techniques in advanced optimization strategies is algorithm optimization, which involves analyzing and optimizing algorithms to improve their efficiency, reduce their time complexity, and minimize their resource usage. Algorithm optimization techniques include algorithmic analysis, algorithmic design paradigms (such as divide and conquer, dynamic programming, and greedy algorithms), algorithmic optimization (such as loop unrolling, caching, and memoization), and algorithmic specialization (such as tailoring algorithms to specific use cases or data distributions). By choosing the right algorithms and optimizing their implementations, developers can achieve significant performance improvements and better utilize system resources.

pythonCopy code

```
# Example code to optimize a sorting algorithm using a more efficient algorithm (e.g., quicksort instead of bubblesort) from random import randint def bubblesort(arr): n = len(arr) for i in range(n): for j in range(0, n-i-1): if arr[j] > arr[j+1]: arr[j], arr[j+1] = arr[j+1], arr[j] def quicksort(arr): if len(arr) <= 1: return arr pivot = arr[len(arr) // 2] left = [x for x in arr if x < pivot] middle = [x for x in arr if x == pivot] right = [x for x in arr if x > pivot] return quicksort(left) + middle + quicksort(right) # Example usage of quicksort algorithm arr = [randint(0, 100) for _ in range(1000)] sorted_arr = quicksort(arr)
```

Code optimization is another crucial aspect of advanced optimization strategies, focusing on improving the performance and efficiency of code by eliminating bottlenecks, reducing redundant computations, and minimizing memory overhead. Code optimization techniques include loop optimization (such as loop unrolling, loop fusion, and loop vectorization), data structure optimization (such as choosing the right data structures for specific use cases and minimizing memory fragmentation), and compiler optimization (such as optimizing compiler flags, inline expansion, and function specialization). By optimizing code at the source code level and leveraging compiler optimizations, developers can achieve significant performance gains without compromising code readability or maintainability.

cCopy code

```
// Example code to optimize a loop using loop unrolling void sum_array(int* arr, int size) { int sum = 0; for (int i = 0; i < size; ++i) { sum += arr[i]; } } // Optimized version using loop unrolling void sum_array_unrolled(int* arr, int size) { int
```

```
sum = 0; for (int i = 0; i < size; i += 4) { sum += arr[i] + arr[i+1] + arr[i+2] + arr[i+3]; } }
```

System optimization techniques focus on optimizing the underlying system infrastructure, including operating systems, runtime environments, and hardware platforms, to improve overall system performance and resource utilization. System optimization techniques include kernel tuning (such as adjusting kernel parameters, scheduling policies, and memory management settings), runtime optimization (such as optimizing garbage collection algorithms, JIT compilation, and runtime libraries), and hardware optimization (such as hardware acceleration, parallel processing, and memory hierarchy optimization). By optimizing the system infrastructure, developers can create a more responsive and efficient runtime environment for their applications, enabling them to achieve better performance and scalability.

bashCopy code

```
# Example command to tune Linux kernel parameters using sysctl sudo sysctl -w kernel.sched_migration_cost_ns=5000000 # Example command to optimize JVM runtime settings using JVM options java -Xmx4g -Xms4g -XX:+UseG1GC -XX:MaxGCPauseMillis=100
```

Architectural optimization focuses on optimizing the overall architecture and design of software applications to improve performance, scalability, and maintainability. Architectural optimization techniques include architectural refactoring (such as breaking monolithic architectures into microservices, optimizing service communication patterns, and minimizing service dependencies), architectural patterns (such as event-driven architecture, reactive architecture, and serverless architecture), and architectural trade-offs (such as balancing performance, scalability, and cost considerations). By adopting a well-designed and optimized architecture, developers can create software applications that are more flexible, scalable, and resilient, enabling them to meet the evolving needs of users and stakeholders.

bashCopy code

```bash
# Example command to deploy a microservices-based architecture using Docker containers docker-compose up -d
```

In summary, advanced optimization strategies are essential for developers striving to maximize the performance, efficiency, and scalability of their software applications. By employing techniques such as algorithm optimization, code optimization, system optimization, and architectural optimization, developers can achieve significant performance gains, deliver faster and more responsive applications, and provide a better user experience to their audience. Advanced optimization strategies require a deep understanding of software engineering principles, performance profiling techniques, and optimization tools, as well as careful consideration of trade-offs and design decisions. By embracing advanced optimization strategies and continuously refining their skills and techniques, developers can create software applications that push the boundaries of performance and efficiency, setting new standards for excellence in the software industry.

BOOK 3

OPTIMIZING PERFORMANCE IN ANDROID STUDIO: EXPERT STRATEGIES FOR EFFICIENT APP DEVELOPMENT

ROB BOTWRIGHT

Chapter 1: Understanding Performance Metrics and Profiling Tools

Performance Metrics Overview is essential for understanding and evaluating the efficiency, reliability, and scalability of software applications across various platforms and environments. Performance metrics encompass a wide range of measurements, indicators, and benchmarks that provide insights into different aspects of an application's performance, including response time, throughput, resource utilization, and error rates. By monitoring and analyzing performance metrics, developers, system administrators, and stakeholders can assess the health and performance of applications, identify performance bottlenecks, and make informed decisions to improve overall system performance and user experience. Performance metrics play a crucial role in software development, deployment, and operations, guiding optimization efforts, capacity planning, and troubleshooting activities to ensure that applications meet performance requirements and deliver a satisfactory user experience.

Response time is one of the most fundamental performance metrics, measuring the time taken by an application to respond to user requests or system events. Response time reflects the overall latency of the system and includes various components such as network latency, server processing time, and client-side rendering time. Monitoring response time allows developers to assess the responsiveness of their applications and identify areas for optimization to reduce latency and improve user experience. Response time can be measured using various tools and techniques, including application performance monitoring

(APM) solutions, network monitoring tools, and custom instrumentation code.

bashCopy code

```
# Example command to measure response time using curl
curl -w "%{time_total}\n" -o /dev/null -s
http://example.com
```

Throughput is another important performance metric, measuring the rate at which a system processes incoming requests or transactions over a given period of time. Throughput indicates the system's capacity to handle concurrent requests and reflects its scalability and resource utilization. Monitoring throughput allows developers to assess the system's capacity limits, identify performance bottlenecks, and optimize resource allocation to improve overall system performance. Throughput can be measured using load testing tools, performance testing frameworks, and monitoring solutions that capture and analyze transaction data in real-time.

bashCopy code

```
# Example command to measure throughput using Apache
Bench ab -n 1000 -c 100 http://example.com/
```

Resource utilization metrics provide insights into the usage of system resources such as CPU, memory, disk I/O, and network bandwidth by an application or system. Monitoring resource utilization allows developers to identify resource bottlenecks, optimize resource allocation, and ensure efficient utilization of available resources. Resource utilization metrics can be collected using system monitoring tools, performance monitoring agents, and cloud-based monitoring services that capture and aggregate resource usage data from across the infrastructure.

bashCopy code

Example command to monitor CPU usage using top top -n 1 -b | grep "Cpu(s)" | awk '{print $2 + $4}'

Error rates are performance metrics that measure the frequency of errors, failures, or exceptions encountered by an application during its operation. Error rates reflect the reliability and stability of the system and indicate the occurrence of issues such as bugs, crashes, or infrastructure failures. Monitoring error rates allows developers to identify and diagnose issues quickly, prioritize bug fixes, and implement preventive measures to reduce the occurrence of errors in the future. Error rates can be tracked using logging frameworks, error monitoring tools, and exception tracking services that capture and analyze error data from application logs and system logs.

bashCopy code

Example command to analyze error rates using grep and awk grep -c "ERROR" /var/log/application.log | awk '{print $1}'

Other performance metrics include availability, which measures the percentage of time that an application or system is operational and accessible to users, and scalability, which measures the system's ability to handle increasing workload or user demand without significant degradation in performance. Availability and scalability are critical performance metrics for mission-critical systems and high-traffic applications, ensuring continuous availability and seamless scalability to meet the needs of users and stakeholders. Monitoring availability and scalability requires implementing redundancy, failover mechanisms, and auto-scaling policies, as well as using monitoring and alerting tools to detect and respond to performance issues in real-time.

In summary, performance metrics are essential for evaluating and optimizing the performance of software applications, enabling developers and system administrators to monitor, analyze, and improve various aspects of system performance, reliability, and scalability. By measuring response time, throughput, resource utilization, error rates, availability, and scalability, organizations can gain insights into the health and performance of their applications and make data-driven decisions to optimize performance, enhance user experience, and achieve business objectives. Performance metrics serve as a foundation for performance engineering practices, enabling continuous improvement and innovation in software development, deployment, and operations.

Profiling Tools Usage in Android Studio is essential for developers aiming to optimize the performance and efficiency of their Android applications. Android Studio, the official integrated development environment (IDE) for Android app development, offers a suite of powerful profiling tools that enable developers to monitor, analyze, and optimize various aspects of their app's performance, including CPU usage, memory usage, network activity, and UI rendering performance. By leveraging these profiling tools, developers can identify performance bottlenecks, memory leaks, and other issues impacting app performance, and take appropriate measures to improve the overall user experience. Profiling tools usage in Android Studio involves a series of steps, including launching the profiler, configuring profiling sessions, capturing performance data, analyzing performance metrics, and interpreting profiling results to identify areas for optimization and improvement.

The Android Profiler is one of the primary profiling tools available in Android Studio, providing real-time insights into key performance metrics of Android applications. To launch the Android Profiler, developers can navigate to the "View" menu in Android Studio, select "Tool Windows," and then choose "Profiler." Alternatively, they can use the keyboard shortcut "Ctrl + Shift + A" to search for actions and commands, and then type "Profiler" to open the Profiler tool window. Once the Profiler is launched, developers can configure profiling sessions to monitor specific performance aspects of their app, such as CPU, memory, network, or energy usage.

bashCopy code

```
# Example command to launch Android Profiler in Android Studio ./studio.sh
```

bashCopy code

```
# Example command to open Android Profiler using keyboard shortcut ctrl + shift + a -> type "Profiler"
```

To configure a profiling session in Android Profiler, developers can select the desired device and app from the device dropdown menu and choose the profiling configuration (e.g., CPU Profiler, Memory Profiler, Network Profiler) from the toolbar. They can then start the profiling session by clicking the "Start" button, which begins capturing performance data from the connected device or emulator. During the profiling session, developers can interact with their app as usual, and Android Profiler will continuously collect performance metrics and display them in real-time on various graphs and charts.

bashCopy code

```
# Example command to start a profiling session in Android Profiler Click on "Start" button in the Profiler toolbar
```

As the profiling session progresses, developers can analyze performance metrics displayed in Android Profiler to identify performance issues and areas for optimization. For example, the CPU Profiler provides insights into CPU usage, thread activity, and method traces, allowing developers to identify

CPU-intensive operations and optimize code execution. The Memory Profiler visualizes memory allocation, garbage collection, and memory leaks, helping developers identify excessive memory usage and memory leaks that may degrade app performance. The Network Profiler captures network activity, including network requests and responses, allowing developers to optimize network usage and minimize latency in network operations.

bashCopy code

```
# Example command to analyze CPU usage in Android Profiler Navigate to CPU Profiler tab and inspect CPU usage graph
```

bashCopy code

```
# Example command to analyze memory allocation in Android Profiler Navigate to Memory Profiler tab and inspect memory allocation graph
```

bashCopy code

```
# Example command to analyze network activity in Android Profiler Navigate to Network Profiler tab and inspect network activity graph
```

In addition to the built-in profiling tools in Android Studio, developers can also use command-line tools such as Systrace and adb shell commands to capture system traces and analyze system behavior and performance. Systrace is a command-line tool that captures system traces of Android devices to analyze system-level events such as CPU scheduling, disk I/O, and graphics rendering. Developers can run Systrace from the command line using the "systrace" command and specify options such as trace duration, output file format, and trace categories to capture detailed system traces for analysis.

bashCopy code

Example command to capture a system trace using Systrace adb shell systrace.py -o trace.html

Similarly, developers can use adb shell commands to collect various performance metrics and diagnostic information from Android devices and emulators, such as CPU usage, memory usage, battery status, and app-specific information. By running adb shell commands such as "top," "dumpsys," and "am," developers can retrieve real-time performance data from the device and diagnose performance issues affecting their apps.

bashCopy code

Example command to retrieve CPU usage information using adb shell adb shell top -n 1

bashCopy code

Example command to retrieve memory usage information using adb shell adb shell dumpsys meminfo com.example.myapp

Overall, profiling tools usage in Android Studio provides developers with invaluable insights into the performance and behavior of their Android applications, enabling them to identify performance bottlenecks, memory leaks, and other issues affecting app performance. By leveraging profiling tools such as Android Profiler, Systrace, and adb shell commands, developers can optimize their apps for better performance, responsiveness, and user experience, ultimately delivering high-quality Android applications to users.

Chapter 2: Memory Management: Avoiding Leaks and Optimizing Memory Usage

Memory Management Fundamentals are crucial for understanding how computer systems allocate, utilize, and release memory resources to run software applications efficiently and effectively. Memory management plays a critical role in modern computing systems, encompassing a range of techniques, algorithms, and mechanisms that govern memory allocation, deallocation, and optimization. By mastering memory management fundamentals, developers, system administrators, and software engineers can optimize memory usage, prevent memory leaks, and improve the overall performance and stability of their software applications. Memory management fundamentals cover various aspects of memory management, including memory allocation strategies, memory models, memory hierarchies, and memory optimization techniques, each contributing to the efficient utilization of system memory and resources.

One of the fundamental aspects of memory management is memory allocation, which involves reserving and assigning memory space to store data and program instructions during program execution. Memory allocation is typically performed dynamically at runtime, allowing programs to request and release memory as needed. Memory allocation strategies include stack allocation and heap allocation, each serving different purposes and offering distinct advantages and limitations. Stack allocation, managed by the runtime stack, is used for storing local variables and function call frames with automatic memory management, while heap allocation, managed by the heap, is used for dynamic memory allocation and data structures with manual memory management.

bashCopy code

```
# Example command to allocate memory dynamically using malloc in C malloc(sizeof(int) * n);
```

pythonCopy code

```
# Example code to allocate memory dynamically using new in C++ new int[n];
```

Memory deallocation is another critical aspect of memory management, involving the release of memory resources that are no longer needed or in use by a program. Memory deallocation prevents memory leaks and ensures that memory resources are efficiently recycled and made available for reuse. Memory deallocation is typically performed manually by the programmer using explicit deallocation functions or automatically by the runtime environment using garbage collection mechanisms. Memory deallocation strategies include explicit deallocation, reference counting, and garbage collection, each offering different trade-offs between performance, simplicity, and memory overhead.

bashCopy code

```
# Example command to deallocate memory using free in C
free(ptr);
```

pythonCopy code

```
# Example code to deallocate memory using delete in C++
delete[] arr;
```

Memory models and memory hierarchies are essential concepts in memory management, defining the organization and structure of memory resources in a computer system. Memory models describe how memory is addressed and accessed by software programs, including flat memory models and segmented memory models. Memory hierarchies describe the arrangement and hierarchy of different types of memory in a computer system, including CPU caches, main memory (RAM), secondary storage (hard disk drives, solid-state drives), and tertiary storage (optical disks, tape drives). Memory models and memory hierarchies influence the performance, latency, and cost of memory operations, and developers must consider them when designing and optimizing software applications.

Memory optimization techniques focus on improving memory usage, efficiency, and performance through various means, including memory pooling, memory fragmentation reduction, and memory compression. Memory pooling involves preallocating and reusing memory blocks from a fixed-size pool to reduce memory allocation overhead and fragmentation. Memory fragmentation reduction techniques aim to minimize memory fragmentation, such as compaction, defragmentation, and memory compaction. Memory compression techniques compress memory contents to reduce memory usage and improve memory efficiency, such as page compression, object compression, and virtual memory compression.

bashCopy code

```
# Example command to create a memory pool in C++
MemoryPool pool(sizeof(int) * n);
```

pythonCopy code

```
# Example code to implement memory pooling in Python
from memory_pool import MemoryPool pool =
MemoryPool()
```

In summary, memory management fundamentals are essential for understanding how computer systems allocate, utilize, and release memory resources to run software applications efficiently and effectively. By mastering memory management fundamentals, developers and system administrators can optimize memory usage, prevent memory leaks, and improve the overall performance and stability of their software applications. Memory management encompasses various techniques, algorithms, and mechanisms, including memory allocation, memory deallocation, memory models, memory hierarchies, and memory optimization techniques, each contributing to the efficient utilization of system memory and resources. By applying memory management principles and best practices, developers can create high-performance, reliable, and scalable software applications that meet the demands of modern computing environments.

Memory Leak Detection and Prevention Techniques are critical for ensuring the stability, reliability, and performance of software applications by identifying and mitigating memory leaks, which occur when a program fails to release memory that is no longer needed, leading to gradual depletion of available memory resources and eventual system instability or failure. Memory leaks can manifest in various forms, including unreleased heap memory, dangling pointers, and orphaned objects, and can occur in any programming language or runtime environment. Detecting and preventing memory leaks requires a combination of techniques, tools, and best practices aimed at identifying memory leaks, diagnosing their root causes, and implementing corrective measures to prevent their recurrence.

One of the primary techniques for memory leak detection is manual code inspection and analysis, which involves reviewing source code, identifying potential memory allocation and deallocation points, and examining memory usage patterns to identify potential memory leaks. Developers can use static code analysis tools, code review practices, and memory profiling tools to identify memory leak-prone code patterns, such as missing deallocation calls, improper memory management, and circular references. By reviewing and analyzing code systematically, developers can proactively identify and fix memory leaks before they impact application performance or stability.

bashCopy code

Example command to perform static code analysis using a linter eslint src/

bashCopy code

Example command to review code changes using a code review tool git diff | review-tool

Memory profiling tools are indispensable for detecting memory leaks in runtime environments by monitoring memory allocation, usage, and deallocation patterns during program execution. Memory profiling tools collect and analyze runtime memory data, such as heap memory usage, object references, and memory allocation events, to identify potential memory leaks and memory usage anomalies. These tools provide insights into memory usage patterns, memory allocation trends, and memory consumption metrics, allowing developers to pinpoint memory leak hotspots and diagnose their root causes effectively.

bashCopy code

Example command to profile memory usage using a memory profiling tool node --inspect-brk app.js

bashCopy code

Example command to analyze memory allocation events using a memory profiler java -jar profiler.jar analyze memory

Dynamic analysis techniques, such as runtime memory instrumentation and memory introspection, enable developers to monitor memory usage and behavior in real-time to detect memory leaks and diagnose memory-related issues as they occur. Runtime memory instrumentation involves injecting code into a running application to monitor memory allocation and usage dynamically, while memory introspection techniques allow developers to inspect memory contents, object references, and memory allocation metadata programmatically to identify memory leaks and diagnose their root causes.

bashCopy code

```
# Example command to instrument memory usage using a memory instrumentation tool npm run start --inspect-memory
```

bashCopy code

```
# Example command to inspect memory contents using memory introspection techniques python memory_inspector.py --process-id 1234
```

Memory leak prevention techniques focus on minimizing the likelihood of memory leaks by adopting best practices, design patterns, and programming techniques that promote efficient memory management and memory usage. Memory leak prevention techniques include using automatic memory management mechanisms, such as garbage collection, smart pointers, and memory-safe languages, to automate memory allocation and deallocation and reduce the risk of memory leaks. Additionally, developers can adopt defensive programming practices, such as null pointer checks, error handling, and resource cleanup routines, to minimize the impact of memory leaks and prevent them from propagating to critical system components.

bashCopy code

```
# Example command to use smart pointers in C++ std::unique_ptr<int> ptr(new int);
```

bashCopy code

Example command to implement error handling in Python try: # Code that may cause memory leaks except Exception as e: # Handle exceptions and clean up resources

Memory leak detection and prevention are ongoing processes that require continuous monitoring, analysis, and improvement to address evolving software requirements and environmental conditions. By integrating memory leak detection and prevention techniques into the software development lifecycle, developers can create more robust, reliable, and resilient software applications that deliver superior performance and stability to end-users. Memory leak detection and prevention should be an integral part of the software development process, with developers incorporating memory management best practices, tools, and techniques into their development workflow to minimize the risk of memory leaks and ensure the long-term health and stability of their applications.

Chapter 3: Optimizing App Startup Time and Launch Performance

App Startup Process Analysis is a critical aspect of software development and performance optimization, focusing on understanding and optimizing the sequence of events that occur when an application is launched. The startup process of an application encompasses various activities, including initialization, configuration loading, resource allocation, and module initialization, each contributing to the overall startup time and user experience. Analyzing the app startup process involves identifying bottlenecks, optimizing critical path operations, and improving startup time to enhance user satisfaction and retention. By analyzing the app startup process, developers can gain insights into the performance characteristics of their applications and identify opportunities for optimization and improvement.

bashCopy code

```bash
# Example command to analyze app startup process using Android Profiler ./gradlew assembleDebug && adb shell am start -S -W com.example.myapp/.MainActivity
```

The first step in app startup process analysis is profiling the startup time to measure the duration of each phase and identify potential performance bottlenecks. Developers can use profiling tools and techniques to capture startup time metrics, such as CPU usage, memory usage, and disk I/O activity, and visualize them using profiling tools such as Android Profiler, Xcode Instruments, or Chrome DevTools. By profiling the startup time, developers can pinpoint areas of the app startup process that contribute most to the overall latency and prioritize optimization efforts accordingly.

bashCopy code

```
# Example command to capture startup time metrics using Xcode Instruments xcodebuild -project MyApp.xcodeproj -scheme MyApp clean build instruments -t "Time Profiler" -w <device_id> MyApp.app
```

Once the startup time metrics have been captured, developers can analyze the data to identify performance bottlenecks and areas for optimization. Common bottlenecks in the app startup process include excessive disk I/O, inefficient resource loading, and blocking operations on the main thread. Developers can use profiling tools to visualize the call stack and identify functions or methods that consume significant CPU time or block the execution of other tasks. By identifying and addressing these bottlenecks, developers can reduce startup time and improve the overall responsiveness of the application.

bashCopy code

```
# Example command to visualize call stack using Chrome DevTools node --inspect-brk app.js
```

Optimizing the app startup process involves implementing various techniques and best practices to streamline initialization, reduce resource contention, and parallelize startup tasks. One common optimization technique is lazy loading, which defers the initialization of non-essential components until they are required, reducing the startup time and memory footprint of the application. Developers can also optimize resource loading by prefetching and caching frequently accessed resources, such as images, fonts, and configuration files, to minimize disk I/O and network latency during startup.

bashCopy code

```
# Example command to prefetch resources using prefetch tags in HTML <link rel="prefetch" href="https://example.com/resource.css">
```

Parallelizing startup tasks is another effective optimization technique, allowing developers to execute independent tasks concurrently to reduce overall startup time. Developers can use multithreading or asynchronous programming techniques to parallelize initialization tasks, such as network requests, database queries, and resource loading, to leverage the multi-core processors available on modern devices and maximize CPU utilization during startup.

bashCopy code

```
# Example command to parallelize network requests using async/await in JavaScript async function fetchData() { const data1 = await fetch('https://api.example.com/data1'); const data2 = await fetch('https://api.example.com/data2'); // Process data1 and data2 concurrently }
```

Monitoring and optimizing memory usage during app startup is essential for ensuring efficient memory allocation and reducing memory overhead. Developers can use memory profiling tools to monitor memory usage patterns and identify memory leaks or excessive memory allocation during startup. By optimizing memory usage and reducing memory fragmentation, developers can improve the overall performance and stability of the application, particularly on memory-constrained devices.

bashCopy code

```bash
# Example command to monitor memory usage using Chrome DevTools Memory panel node --inspect app.js
```

In summary, app startup process analysis is a critical step in software development and performance optimization, enabling developers to understand the performance characteristics of their applications and identify opportunities for optimization and improvement. By profiling the startup time, analyzing performance bottlenecks, and implementing optimization techniques, developers can reduce startup time, improve user satisfaction, and deliver a better overall user experience. App startup process analysis should be an integral part of the software development lifecycle, with developers continuously monitoring and optimizing the startup performance of their applications to ensure optimal performance and responsiveness.

Strategies for Accelerating App Launch Time are essential for ensuring that users have a seamless and responsive experience when launching mobile and web applications. App launch time refers to the duration it takes for an application to start up and become usable after the user initiates the launch process. Accelerating app launch time is crucial for enhancing user satisfaction, reducing user churn, and improving overall app performance. There are various strategies and techniques that developers can employ to optimize app launch time and deliver a faster and more responsive user experience.

Profiling the app launch process is the first step in identifying areas for optimization. Developers can use profiling tools and techniques to measure the duration of each phase of the app launch process and identify performance bottlenecks. Profiling tools such as Android Profiler, Xcode Instruments, and Chrome DevTools provide insights into CPU usage, memory usage, disk I/O activity, and network activity during the app launch process. By profiling the app launch process, developers can pinpoint areas of inefficiency and prioritize optimization efforts to reduce app launch time.

bashCopy code

```
# Example command to profile app launch time using Android Profiler ./gradlew assembleDebug && adb shell am start -S -W com.example.myapp/.MainActivity
```

bashCopy code

```
# Example command to profile app launch time using Xcode Instruments xcodebuild -project MyApp.xcodeproj -scheme MyApp clean build instruments -t "Time Profiler" -w <device_id> MyApp.app
```

Optimizing resource loading is a common strategy for accelerating app launch time. Developers can reduce app launch time by prefetching and caching resources such as images, fonts, and configuration files that are required during the app launch process. By prefetching resources, developers can minimize disk I/O and network latency during app launch, leading to a faster and more responsive user experience. Developers can use techniques such as lazy loading and resource bundling to optimize resource loading and reduce app launch time.

bashCopy code

```
# Example command to prefetch resources using prefetch tags in HTML <link rel="prefetch" href="https://example.com/resource.css">
```

Parallelizing initialization tasks is another effective strategy for accelerating app launch time. Developers can parallelize initialization tasks such as network requests, database queries, and resource loading to leverage the multi-core processors available on modern devices and maximize CPU utilization during app launch. By parallelizing initialization tasks, developers can reduce the overall duration of the app launch process and improve the responsiveness of the application.

bashCopy code

```
# Example command to parallelize network requests using async/await in JavaScript async function fetchData() { const data1 = await fetch('https://api.example.com/data1'); const data2 = await fetch('https://api.example.com/data2'); // Process data1 and data2 concurrently }
```

Optimizing memory usage is essential for accelerating app launch time and improving overall app performance. Developers can optimize memory usage by reducing memory overhead, minimizing memory fragmentation, and optimizing memory allocation and deallocation. By optimizing memory usage, developers can reduce the memory footprint of the application and improve the efficiency of memory operations during the app launch process. Memory profiling tools can help developers identify memory leaks, excessive memory allocation, and memory fragmentation issues that may impact app launch time.

bashCopy code

```
# Example command to monitor memory usage using Chrome DevTools Memory panel node --inspect app.js
```

Reducing startup time is a critical aspect of accelerating app launch time. Developers can optimize startup time by minimizing the number of dependencies, reducing code complexity, and optimizing critical path operations during app initialization. By reducing startup time, developers can improve the overall responsiveness of the application and enhance the user experience.

In summary, accelerating app launch time is crucial for delivering a fast, responsive, and engaging user experience. By profiling the app launch process, optimizing resource loading, parallelizing initialization tasks, optimizing memory usage, and reducing startup time, developers can significantly improve app launch time and enhance user satisfaction. Accelerating app launch time should be an integral part of the app development process, with developers continuously monitoring and optimizing app launch performance to ensure optimal performance and responsiveness.

UI Thread Optimization Techniques are essential for ensuring smooth and responsive user interfaces in software applications, especially in mobile and web environments where user experience is paramount. The UI thread, also known as the main thread or the UI thread, is responsible for handling user interactions, updating the user interface, and responding to user input. However, performing complex or time-consuming operations on the UI thread can lead to sluggishness, unresponsiveness, and poor user experience. To address these issues, developers can employ various optimization techniques to streamline UI thread performance, improve responsiveness, and deliver a seamless user experience.

One of the primary UI thread optimization techniques is offloading long-running or computationally intensive tasks to background threads or worker threads. By delegating tasks such as network requests, database queries, and image processing to background threads, developers can prevent blocking the UI thread and ensure that the user interface remains responsive and fluid. In Android development, developers can use the AsyncTask class or Kotlin coroutines to perform asynchronous operations on background threads and update the UI thread with the results.

bashCopy code

```
# Example command to perform asynchronous operation using AsyncTask in Android AsyncTask.execute(() -> { // Perform background operation return result; });
```

bashCopy code

```
# Example command to perform asynchronous operation using Kotlin coroutines in Android GlobalScope.launch(Dispatchers.IO) { // Perform background operation val result = fetchData() withContext(Dispatchers.Main) { // Update UI with result } }
```

Another UI thread optimization technique is minimizing UI thread contention by reducing the frequency and duration of UI thread operations. Developers can optimize UI performance by batching UI updates, minimizing layout changes, and reducing the number of view redraws. For example, developers can batch multiple UI updates into a single request using the requestLayout() and invalidate() methods in Android, or by using the setNeedsLayout() and setNeedsDisplay() methods in iOS. Additionally, developers can optimize layout performance by using lightweight layout containers, optimizing view hierarchy depth, and avoiding nested layouts.

bashCopy code

```
# Example command to batch UI updates in Android viewGroup.requestLayout(); viewGroup.invalidate();
```

bashCopy code

```
# Example command to batch UI updates in iOS view.setNeedsLayout(); view.setNeedsDisplay();
```

Caching UI resources and preloading data is another effective UI thread optimization technique for improving responsiveness and reducing UI latency. By caching frequently used UI resources such as images, fonts, and layouts, developers can minimize disk I/O and network latency during UI rendering. Additionally, developers can preload data and UI components in advance to reduce loading times and improve the perceived responsiveness of the application. In Android development, developers can use libraries such as Glide or Picasso for image caching and preloading, while in iOS development, developers can use libraries such as SDWebImage or Kingfisher.

bashCopy code

```
# Example command to preload data in Android
Glide.with(context).load("https://example.com/image.jpg").preload();
```

bashCopy code

```
# Example command to preload data in iOS
SDWebImageManager.shared().loadImage(with: URL(string: "https://example.com/image.jpg"), options: .preload, context: nil, progress: nil, completed: nil)
```

Optimizing UI rendering performance is crucial for delivering smooth and fluid user interfaces. Developers can optimize UI rendering performance by reducing overdraw, minimizing view complexity, and optimizing layout performance. Overdraw occurs when multiple views are drawn on top of each other, resulting in unnecessary GPU rendering overhead. Developers can reduce overdraw by optimizing view hierarchy, flattening view layers, and using hardware-accelerated rendering techniques such as hardware layers or render caches. Additionally, developers can optimize layout performance by using lightweight layout containers, optimizing view measurement and layout, and avoiding excessive nested layouts.

bashCopy code

Example command to enable hardware acceleration in Android android:hardwareAccelerated="true"
bashCopy code
Example command to enable hardware acceleration in iOS view.layer.shouldRasterize = true
In summary, UI thread optimization techniques are essential for ensuring smooth, responsive, and fluid user interfaces in software applications. By offloading long-running tasks to background threads, minimizing UI thread contention, caching UI resources, preloading data, and optimizing UI rendering performance, developers can improve UI thread performance, reduce UI latency, and deliver a superior user experience. UI thread optimization should be an integral part of the software development process, with developers continuously monitoring and optimizing UI performance to ensure optimal responsiveness and usability.

Improving UI Performance with RenderThread is a critical aspect of modern application development, particularly in the realm of mobile and web applications where user experience is paramount. The RenderThread, also known as the render pipeline or rendering thread, is responsible for rendering the user interface and processing UI updates in an efficient and responsive manner. By leveraging the capabilities of the RenderThread, developers can significantly enhance UI performance, reduce rendering latency, and deliver a smooth and fluid user experience.
One of the primary benefits of using RenderThread for UI rendering is the ability to offload rendering operations from the main UI thread, also known as the UI or main thread. Offloading rendering operations to the

RenderThread allows the UI thread to remain responsive and handle user interactions without being blocked by rendering tasks. This separation of rendering and UI logic helps prevent UI jank, stuttering, and unresponsiveness, particularly during complex or resource-intensive rendering operations such as animations, transitions, and complex layouts.

bashCopy code

```
# Example command to enable RenderThread acceleration in Android adb shell setprop debug.hwui.renderer skiavk
```

Another advantage of using RenderThread for UI rendering is improved rendering performance and efficiency. The RenderThread is optimized for rendering tasks and utilizes hardware acceleration and multithreading techniques to maximize rendering performance and minimize rendering latency. By leveraging the capabilities of the RenderThread, developers can achieve smoother animations, faster UI rendering, and improved overall UI performance, leading to a more responsive and engaging user experience.

bashCopy code

```
# Example command to profile rendering performance using Android Profiler ./gradlew assembleDebug && adb shell am start -S -W com.example.myapp/.MainActivity
```

RenderThread also provides better synchronization and coordination between UI updates and rendering operations, ensuring that UI changes are reflected on the screen promptly and accurately. Unlike traditional rendering models where UI updates are processed sequentially on the UI thread, RenderThread processes rendering commands asynchronously, allowing for more efficient use of system resources and smoother UI transitions. This asynchronous rendering model helps minimize UI latency, reduce frame drops, and improve the overall responsiveness of the application.

bashCopy code

```
# Example command to optimize UI transitions using RenderThread in Android ValueAnimator animator = ValueAnimator.ofFloat(0f, 1f); animator.setDuration(300); animator.addUpdateListener(animation -> { // Update UI with animation progress }); animator.start();
```

Moreover, RenderThread enables better utilization of hardware acceleration and graphics processing units (GPUs) for UI rendering. By leveraging hardware acceleration capabilities, such as OpenGL ES or Vulkan APIs, RenderThread can offload rendering tasks to the GPU, allowing for faster and more efficient rendering of complex UI elements, animations, and effects. This hardware-accelerated rendering approach enhances UI performance, reduces CPU overhead, and improves energy efficiency, particularly on devices with dedicated graphics hardware.

bashCopy code

```
# Example command to enable hardware acceleration in Android android:hardwareAccelerated="true"
```

In addition to improving rendering performance, RenderThread also provides better support for advanced UI features and effects, such as dynamic shadows, motion blur, and particle effects. These advanced UI features require real-time rendering capabilities and efficient utilization of system resources, which RenderThread can provide through hardware acceleration and multithreading techniques. By leveraging RenderThread for UI rendering, developers can implement rich and immersive user interfaces with advanced graphical effects and animations, enhancing the overall user experience and visual appeal of their applications.

bashCopy code

```bash
# Example command to implement dynamic shadows using RenderThread in Android View.setElevation(10);
```

In summary, improving UI performance with RenderThread is essential for delivering smooth, responsive, and visually appealing user interfaces in modern applications. By offloading rendering operations to the RenderThread, optimizing rendering performance, leveraging hardware acceleration, and supporting advanced UI features, developers can achieve faster rendering, reduced UI latency, and improved overall UI performance. RenderThread should be an integral part of the UI rendering pipeline, with developers continuously optimizing and fine-tuning UI performance to ensure optimal responsiveness and user experience.

Chapter 5: Managing Battery Consumption and Power Efficiency

Battery Consumption Analysis Tools are crucial for developers seeking to optimize the energy efficiency of their applications, especially in mobile and portable device environments where battery life is a critical factor. These tools provide insights into how applications consume battery power, identify energy-intensive operations, and suggest optimizations to reduce battery consumption. By using battery consumption analysis tools, developers can diagnose and address battery drain issues, improve energy efficiency, and enhance the overall user experience of their applications.

One of the prominent battery consumption analysis tools widely used by developers is the Android Battery Historian tool. Android Battery Historian allows developers to analyze battery usage data collected from Android devices and visualize battery consumption patterns over time. Developers can use Battery Historian to identify energy-intensive app components, such as wake locks, background services, and network activity, and evaluate their impact on battery life. By analyzing battery usage statistics, developers can pinpoint areas for optimization and implement energy-saving strategies to reduce battery consumption.

bashCopy code

```
# Example command to capture battery usage data using adb adb shell dumpsys batterystats --reset adb shell dumpsys batterystats --charged
```

Another battery consumption analysis tool commonly used by developers is the Battery Usage Monitor in iOS devices.

The Battery Usage Monitor provides insights into how apps and system services consume battery power on iOS devices and identifies energy-intensive apps and processes. Developers can use the Battery Usage Monitor to track battery usage statistics, monitor app background activity, and identify apps with high energy impact. By analyzing battery usage data, developers can identify energy-hungry apps and optimize their energy consumption to improve battery life.

bashCopy code

```
# Example command to view battery usage statistics on iOS devices Settings -> Battery -> Battery Usage
```

In addition to platform-specific battery consumption analysis tools, developers can use third-party battery profiling tools and libraries to analyze battery usage across multiple platforms and devices. One such tool is the Battery Historian web tool, which provides a web-based interface for visualizing battery usage data collected from Android devices. Developers can upload battery usage data to the Battery Historian web tool and analyze battery consumption patterns, identify energy-intensive app components, and evaluate the impact of optimizations on battery life. By using third-party battery profiling tools, developers can gain cross-platform insights into battery consumption and optimize their applications for improved energy efficiency.

bashCopy code

```
# Example command to upload battery usage data to Battery Historian web tool python historian.py <battery_usage_data_file>
```

Battery consumption analysis tools typically provide detailed insights into various aspects of battery usage, including CPU usage, network activity, wake locks, and sensor usage. Developers can use these insights to identify energy-intensive app components and optimize their energy consumption to reduce battery drain. For example, developers can minimize background activity, reduce CPU and network usage, optimize data synchronization, and implement efficient power management techniques to improve energy efficiency and extend battery life.

bashCopy code

```
# Example command to analyze CPU usage using Battery Historian python historian.py --show_cpu_time <battery_usage_data_file>
```

Moreover, battery consumption analysis tools often provide recommendations and best practices for optimizing energy consumption and improving battery life. These recommendations may include reducing the frequency of background tasks, optimizing resource usage, using platform-specific energy-saving features, and leveraging power management APIs provided by the operating system. By following these recommendations and implementing energy-saving strategies, developers can optimize their applications for improved battery efficiency and deliver a better user experience to their users.

bashCopy code

```
# Example command to view recommendations for battery optimization Battery Historian web tool -> Recommendations tab
```

In summary, battery consumption analysis tools are essential for developers seeking to optimize the energy efficiency of their applications and improve battery life. By using these tools, developers can analyze battery usage data, identify energy-intensive app components, and implement optimizations to reduce battery drain. Battery consumption analysis should be an integral part of the application development process, with developers continuously monitoring and optimizing battery usage to deliver energy-efficient applications and enhance the overall user experience.

Power Efficiency Best Practices are crucial for developers aiming to create energy-efficient software applications, especially in the context of mobile and portable devices where battery life is a significant concern. These best practices encompass a range of techniques and strategies that developers can employ to minimize power consumption, extend battery life, and reduce environmental impact. By adhering to power efficiency best practices, developers can optimize the energy efficiency of their applications, improve user experience, and contribute to sustainability efforts.

One of the fundamental power efficiency best practices is to minimize CPU and GPU utilization. High CPU and GPU usage can significantly impact battery life, as these components consume a considerable amount of power. Developers can optimize CPU and GPU utilization by reducing the frequency and duration of CPU-intensive tasks, such as background computation, rendering, and animation. By minimizing CPU and GPU usage, developers can reduce power consumption and extend battery life, leading to a better user experience and improved energy efficiency.

Another essential best practice for power efficiency is to optimize network usage. Network communication, such as Wi-Fi, cellular data, and Bluetooth, can consume a significant amount of power, especially when operating in high-power modes or continuously transferring data. Developers can optimize network usage by minimizing the frequency and size of network requests, using efficient data synchronization techniques, and leveraging platform-specific energy-saving features, such as Wi-Fi offloading and background network limitations. By optimizing network usage, developers can reduce power consumption and improve battery life without compromising application functionality.

bashCopy code

```
# Example command to optimize network usage in Android
Settings -> Network & internet -> Wi-Fi -> Wi-Fi preferences
-> Wi-Fi offloading
```

Optimizing screen brightness and display settings is another effective power efficiency best practice. The display is one of the most power-hungry components of a device, and adjusting screen brightness and display settings can have a significant impact on battery life. Developers can optimize screen brightness by using adaptive brightness algorithms, adjusting screen brightness dynamically based on ambient light conditions, and implementing dark mode or low-power display modes. Additionally, developers can encourage users to adjust display settings manually or provide options for customizing display brightness and timeout settings to optimize power consumption.

bashCopy code

```
# Example command to adjust display settings in Android
Settings -> Display -> Brightness level
```

Reducing background activity and optimizing power management are critical power efficiency best practices for improving battery life. Background processes, such as background services, location tracking, and push notifications, can consume a considerable amount of power, even when the device is idle. Developers can optimize power management by minimizing background activity, limiting the frequency of background tasks, and implementing efficient background processing techniques, such as batch processing and deferred synchronization. Additionally, developers can leverage platform-specific power management features, such as Doze mode in Android or Low Power Mode in iOS, to further reduce power consumption during idle periods.

bashCopy code

```
# Example command to enable Doze mode in Android adb shell dumpsys deviceidle enable
```

Efficiently managing device sensors, such as GPS, accelerometer, and gyroscope, is essential for power efficiency. Sensors consume power when active, and unnecessary sensor polling can drain the battery quickly. Developers can optimize sensor usage by minimizing sensor polling frequency, using sensor batching and fusion techniques to reduce power consumption, and implementing sensor algorithms that intelligently detect and respond to changes in sensor data. By efficiently managing device sensors, developers can minimize power consumption and improve battery life without sacrificing sensor functionality.

bashCopy code

```
# Example command to manage sensor usage in Android Settings -> Location -> Advanced -> Google Location Accuracy
```

Lastly, optimizing app architecture and resource usage is a fundamental power efficiency best practice. Bloated app architectures, excessive resource usage, and inefficient coding practices can contribute to high power consumption and reduced battery life. Developers can optimize app architecture by using lightweight frameworks and libraries, minimizing memory usage, and optimizing resource loading and caching. Additionally, developers can employ techniques such as lazy loading, resource pooling, and object pooling to minimize resource overhead and improve energy efficiency. By optimizing app architecture and resource usage, developers can reduce power consumption, improve battery life, and deliver a more responsive and energy-efficient user experience.

bashCopy code

```
# Example command to optimize memory usage in Android
adb shell dumpsys meminfo <package_name>
```

In summary, power efficiency best practices are essential for developers seeking to optimize the energy efficiency of their applications and improve battery life. By adhering to these best practices, developers can minimize CPU and GPU utilization, optimize network usage, adjust display settings, reduce background activity, manage device sensors efficiently, and optimize app architecture and resource usage. Power efficiency should be a primary consideration throughout the software development lifecycle, with developers continuously monitoring and optimizing power consumption to deliver energy-efficient applications and improve user experience.

Chapter 6: Network Performance Optimization: Minimizing Data Usage and Latency

Network Performance Metrics Overview is crucial for developers and network administrators seeking to monitor and optimize the performance of their network infrastructure and applications. Network performance metrics provide insights into the speed, reliability, and efficiency of data transfer across network devices and protocols. By monitoring network performance metrics, organizations can identify bottlenecks, troubleshoot issues, and optimize network configuration to ensure optimal performance and reliability.

One of the fundamental network performance metrics is bandwidth, which refers to the maximum rate at which data can be transferred between network devices. Bandwidth is typically measured in bits per second (bps) or its derivatives, such as kilobits per second (Kbps), megabits per second (Mbps), and gigabits per second (Gbps). Bandwidth represents the capacity of the network link and determines the maximum data transfer rate achievable between two points in the network. Higher bandwidth allows for faster data transfer speeds and better network performance.

bashCopy code

```bash
# Example command to measure bandwidth using iperf tool
iperf -c <server_ip_address>
```

Latency is another critical network performance metric that measures the time it takes for a data packet to travel from its source to its destination and back. Latency is typically measured in milliseconds (ms) and represents the round-trip time (RTT) between network devices. Lower latency indicates faster response times and better network responsiveness, while higher latency can result in delays, jitter, and degraded user experience. Monitoring latency is essential for real-time applications such as VoIP, video conferencing, and online gaming, where low latency is crucial for optimal performance.

bashCopy code

```
# Example command to measure latency using ping tool
ping <destination_ip_address>
```

Packet loss is another important network performance metric that measures the percentage of data packets lost or dropped during transmission across the network. Packet loss can occur due to network congestion, hardware failures, or transmission errors and can have a significant impact on application performance and user experience. High packet loss rates can result in retransmissions, increased latency, and degraded network performance. Monitoring packet loss is essential for identifying network issues and optimizing network configuration to minimize packet loss and improve reliability.

bashCopy code

```
# Example command to measure packet loss using traceroute tool traceroute <destination_ip_address>
```

Throughput is a network performance metric that measures the actual data transfer rate achieved between network devices. Unlike bandwidth, which represents the theoretical maximum data transfer rate, throughput reflects the actual data transfer rate observed in real-world network conditions. Throughput is influenced by various factors, including bandwidth, latency, packet loss, and network congestion. Monitoring throughput helps organizations evaluate network performance, identify performance bottlenecks, and optimize network configuration to maximize data transfer efficiency.

```
bashCopy code
# Example command to measure throughput using iperf tool
iperf -c <server_ip_address>
```

Network reliability is another critical network performance metric that measures the ability of the network to deliver data packets accurately and consistently. Reliability is typically expressed as a percentage and represents the likelihood that data packets will be delivered successfully without errors or loss. High network reliability ensures data integrity, reduces the risk of data loss or corruption, and enhances user experience. Monitoring network reliability helps organizations identify potential issues and implement measures to improve network stability and resilience.

```
bashCopy code
# Example command to measure network reliability using ping tool ping -c <number_of_packets> <destination_ip_address>
```

In addition to these primary network performance metrics, there are several other metrics that organizations may monitor to assess network performance and health. These include network congestion, jitter, retransmission rate, error rate, and Quality of Service (QoS) parameters such as latency variation and packet delivery ratio. By monitoring these metrics and analyzing network performance data, organizations can gain insights into network behavior, detect anomalies, and take proactive measures to optimize network performance and reliability.

```
bashCopy code
# Example command to measure network congestion using netstat tool netstat -s
```

Overall, network performance metrics play a crucial role in assessing the performance, reliability, and efficiency of network infrastructure and applications. By monitoring key network performance metrics such as bandwidth, latency, packet loss, throughput, and reliability, organizations can identify performance bottlenecks, troubleshoot issues, and optimize network configuration to ensure optimal performance and user experience. Network performance monitoring should be an integral part of network management and administration, with organizations continuously monitoring and analyzing network performance data to maintain network health and efficiency.

Techniques for Minimizing Data Usage and Latency are essential for developers and network administrators striving to optimize the performance and efficiency of their applications and network infrastructure. In today's data-driven world, where users expect fast and responsive applications with minimal data usage, minimizing data usage and latency has become paramount. By employing various techniques and strategies, developers and network administrators can reduce data consumption, minimize latency, and enhance the overall user experience.
One of the fundamental techniques for minimizing data usage and latency is data compression. Data compression reduces the size of data packets transmitted over the network by eliminating redundant information and encoding data more efficiently. By compressing data before transmission, developers can reduce the amount of data transferred over the network, leading to lower bandwidth usage and reduced latency. There are several compression algorithms available, such as gzip, deflate, and Brotli, which developers can integrate into their applications to compress data before sending it over the network.
bashCopy code

Example command to compress data using gzip gzip <file_name>

Caching is another effective technique for minimizing data usage and latency. Caching involves storing frequently accessed data locally on the client or server side, allowing subsequent requests for the same data to be served from the cache instead of fetching it from the original source. By caching data, developers can reduce the number of network requests, minimize data transfer, and improve application responsiveness. Developers can implement caching using various techniques, such as browser caching, server-side caching, and content delivery networks (CDNs), to store and serve cached data efficiently.

bashCopy code

Example command to enable browser caching in Apache HTTP Server Header set Cache-Control "max-age=3600, public"

Optimizing network protocols and communication is essential for minimizing data usage and latency. Developers can optimize network protocols by choosing lightweight and efficient protocols, such as HTTP/2 or WebSocket, that minimize protocol overhead and improve data transfer efficiency. Additionally, developers can optimize network communication by reducing the number of round trips, minimizing header size, and using multiplexing and pipelining techniques to combine multiple requests into a single connection. By optimizing network protocols and communication, developers can reduce latency and improve data transfer efficiency, leading to faster and more responsive applications.

bashCopy code

Example command to enable HTTP/2 protocol in Apache HTTP Server Protocols h2 http/1.1

Implementing data prefetching and preloading techniques can also help minimize data usage and latency. Data prefetching involves proactively fetching and caching data before it is requested by the user, anticipating user actions and reducing the time required to load data dynamically. Preloading, on the other hand, involves loading essential resources, such as images, scripts, and stylesheets, in advance to reduce latency and improve page load times. By prefetching and preloading data, developers can minimize network latency, improve data availability, and enhance the overall user experience.

bashCopy code

```
# Example command to prefetch data using HTML link prefetching <link rel="prefetch" href="example.html">
```

Reducing unnecessary data transfer and optimizing resource usage are key strategies for minimizing data usage and latency. Developers can optimize resource usage by minimizing the size of resources, such as images, videos, and scripts, using compression techniques, such as image optimization and minification, to reduce file size without sacrificing quality. Additionally, developers can reduce unnecessary data transfer by implementing lazy loading and deferred loading techniques to load resources only when needed, reducing initial page load times and conserving bandwidth.

bashCopy code

```
# Example command to optimize images using ImageMagick
convert input.jpg -resize 50% output.jpg
```

Lastly, leveraging content delivery networks (CDNs) and edge caching services can help minimize data usage and latency by distributing content closer to end users and reducing the distance data needs to travel. CDNs cache content on servers located at strategic locations worldwide, allowing users to access content from the nearest server, reducing latency and improving data transfer efficiency. By integrating CDNs into their applications, developers can minimize data usage, reduce latency, and improve the overall user experience for users accessing their applications from different geographic locations.

bashCopy code

```bash
# Example command to configure CDN caching rules in Cloudflare Cache-Control: max-age=3600, public
```

In summary, techniques for minimizing data usage and latency are essential for optimizing the performance and efficiency of applications and network infrastructure. By employing techniques such as data compression, caching, protocol optimization, data prefetching, resource optimization, and CDN integration, developers and network administrators can reduce data consumption, minimize latency, and improve the overall user experience. Minimizing data usage and latency should be a primary consideration in application development and network optimization, with developers continuously monitoring and optimizing data transfer and latency to ensure optimal performance and user satisfaction.

Chapter 7: Database Performance Tuning and Query Optimization

Database Performance Metrics Overview provides insights into the performance and efficiency of database systems, essential for administrators and developers managing large-scale data environments. Monitoring database performance metrics is critical for ensuring optimal performance, identifying bottlenecks, and troubleshooting issues that can affect the overall system's responsiveness and reliability. By analyzing key database performance metrics, administrators and developers can optimize database configurations, improve query performance, and enhance the user experience.

One of the fundamental database performance metrics is throughput, which measures the rate at which data is processed and transmitted by the database system. Throughput is typically measured in transactions per second (TPS) or queries per second (QPS) and represents the system's capacity to handle incoming requests efficiently. Monitoring throughput helps administrators assess the system's overall performance and scalability, identify peak usage periods, and plan capacity upgrades or optimizations to accommodate increasing workloads.

bashCopy code

```bash
# Example command to measure database throughput using database monitoring tools like Prometheus and Grafana
```

Latency is another critical database performance metric that measures the time taken for a database operation to complete, typically measured in milliseconds (ms). Latency includes various components, such as network latency, disk latency, and query processing time, and reflects the system's responsiveness to user requests. High latency can result in slow query execution times, delayed data retrieval, and degraded application performance. Monitoring latency helps administrators identify performance bottlenecks, optimize query execution plans, and improve overall system responsiveness.

bashCopy code

```
# Example command to measure database latency using SQL query execution time SELECT * FROM table_name;
```

Concurrency is a database performance metric that measures the system's ability to handle multiple concurrent transactions or queries simultaneously. Concurrency is essential for ensuring efficient resource utilization and avoiding contention for system resources, such as CPU, memory, and disk I/O. Monitoring concurrency helps administrators identify potential bottlenecks, such as locking and blocking issues, and optimize database configurations to improve concurrency and throughput.

bashCopy code

```
# Example command to monitor database concurrency using database management tools like MySQL Workbench or pgAdmin
```

Resource utilization is another important database performance metric that measures the system's usage of hardware resources, such as CPU, memory, disk I/O, and network bandwidth. Monitoring resource utilization helps administrators identify resource-intensive queries or operations, detect potential performance bottlenecks, and allocate resources efficiently to ensure optimal system performance. Administrators can use various monitoring tools and utilities to track resource utilization metrics in real-time and identify opportunities for optimization.

bashCopy code

```
# Example command to monitor database resource utilization using operating system utilities like top (Linux) or Task Manager (Windows)
```

Query execution time is a database performance metric that measures the time taken for individual queries to execute, typically measured in milliseconds (ms) or seconds (s). Monitoring query execution time helps administrators identify slow-running queries, inefficient query execution plans, and performance bottlenecks that can affect overall system performance. By analyzing query execution times, administrators can optimize query performance, create appropriate indexes, and tune database configurations to improve overall system responsiveness.

bashCopy code

```
# Example command to monitor query execution time using database query profiling tools like EXPLAIN (MySQL) or EXPLAIN ANALYZE (PostgreSQL)
```

Database availability is a critical performance metric that measures the system's uptime and reliability, typically expressed as a percentage. High availability ensures that the database system remains accessible and operational, even in the event of hardware failures, software errors, or network outages. Monitoring database availability helps administrators identify potential issues, such as system failures or downtime, and implement measures to ensure continuous availability and data integrity.

bashCopy code

Example command to monitor database availability using database monitoring tools like Nagios or Zabbix

Data consistency is another important database performance metric that measures the accuracy and integrity of data stored in the database. Consistent data ensures that transactions are processed correctly and that the database reflects the latest changes made by users or applications. Monitoring data consistency helps administrators detect anomalies, such as data corruption or synchronization errors, and implement measures to maintain data integrity and consistency across the database system.

bashCopy code

Example command to monitor data consistency using database integrity checks or checksum validation tools

Scalability is a database performance metric that measures the system's ability to handle increasing workloads and data volumes without sacrificing performance or reliability. Scalability is essential for accommodating growing user bases, increasing transaction volumes, and expanding data storage requirements. Monitoring scalability helps administrators assess the system's capacity limits, identify potential scalability bottlenecks, and implement scaling strategies, such as vertical or horizontal scaling, to ensure continued performance and reliability as the system grows.

bashCopy code

Example command to monitor database scalability using load testing tools like Apache JMeter or Gatling

In summary, database performance metrics are essential for monitoring and optimizing the performance and efficiency of database systems. By analyzing key performance metrics such as throughput, latency, concurrency, resource utilization, query execution time, availability, data consistency, and scalability, administrators can identify performance bottlenecks, optimize database configurations, and ensure optimal system performance and reliability. Monitoring database performance should be an ongoing process, with administrators continuously monitoring performance metrics, identifying areas for improvement, and implementing optimizations to ensure optimal database performance and user satisfaction.

Query Optimization Strategies are crucial for database administrators and developers seeking to improve the performance and efficiency of database queries, essential for ensuring fast and responsive data retrieval in database-driven applications. Optimizing queries involves analyzing and fine-tuning SQL queries to reduce execution time, minimize resource utilization, and improve overall system performance. By employing various optimization techniques and strategies, administrators and developers can enhance query performance, optimize database operations, and deliver a better user experience.
One of the fundamental query optimization strategies is indexing, which involves creating indexes on database tables to facilitate faster data retrieval and query execution. Indexes are data structures that store a sorted copy of selected columns from a table, allowing the database engine to quickly locate and retrieve rows matching specific criteria. By creating indexes on columns frequently used in WHERE clauses, JOIN conditions, and ORDER BY clauses, administrators can significantly

improve query performance and reduce the time required to retrieve data from the database.

bashCopy code

```
# Example command to create an index in SQL CREATE INDEX index_name ON table_name(column_name);
```

Another important query optimization strategy is table partitioning, which involves dividing large database tables into smaller, more manageable partitions based on predefined criteria, such as range, list, or hash. Partitioning helps distribute data across multiple storage devices or disk volumes, improving query performance by reducing the amount of data that needs to be scanned and processed for each query. By partitioning tables based on access patterns, administrators can improve query performance, optimize storage efficiency, and streamline database maintenance operations.

bashCopy code

```
# Example command to partition a table in SQL ALTER TABLE table_name PARTITION BY RANGE(column_name);
```

Query rewriting is a technique used to rewrite or refactor complex SQL queries into simpler, more efficient forms without altering their intended functionality. By analyzing query execution plans, identifying inefficient query patterns, and optimizing query syntax and structure, administrators can improve query performance and reduce resource utilization. Query rewriting techniques include simplifying JOIN operations, eliminating unnecessary subqueries, and optimizing predicate filtering conditions to minimize the number of rows processed by the database engine.

bashCopy code

Example command to rewrite a complex SQL query SELECT * FROM table1 JOIN table2 ON table1.id = table2.id WHERE condition;

Using appropriate query hints and directives is another effective query optimization strategy for influencing the behavior of the database optimizer and execution engine. Query hints provide instructions to the database optimizer on how to execute a particular query, such as specifying index hints, join hints, or query execution plans. By providing hints to the optimizer, administrators can influence query execution strategies, improve query performance, and address performance bottlenecks without modifying the underlying SQL code.

bashCopy code

```
# Example command to provide query hints in SQL SELECT /*+ INDEX(table_name index_name) */ column_name FROM table_name;
```

Database administrators can also optimize query performance by analyzing and tuning database configuration parameters, such as memory allocation, disk I/O settings, and query optimization thresholds. By adjusting database configuration settings, administrators can optimize resource utilization, improve query execution times, and enhance overall system performance. Common database configuration tuning techniques include adjusting memory buffer sizes, optimizing disk read/write operations, and fine-tuning query optimizer parameters to better suit specific workload characteristics.

bashCopy code

Example command to tune database configuration parameters in MySQL SET GLOBAL variable_name = value;

Query caching is a technique used to cache the results of frequently executed queries in memory or on disk, allowing subsequent identical queries to be served from the cache instead of re-executing the query against the database. By caching query results, administrators can reduce query execution times, minimize database load, and improve overall system performance. Query caching is particularly effective for read-heavy workloads and applications with repetitive data access patterns.

bashCopy code

```
# Example command to enable query caching in MySQL
SET GLOBAL query_cache_size = size;
```

Database administrators can optimize query performance by partitioning data across multiple physical or virtual servers using techniques such as sharding or replication. Sharding involves horizontally partitioning database tables into smaller subsets, distributing data across multiple servers based on predefined criteria, such as customer ID or geographic location. Replication involves creating copies of database tables on multiple servers, allowing read-heavy workloads to be distributed across replicas to improve query performance and scalability.

bashCopy code

```
# Example command to enable sharding in MongoDB
sh.enableSharding(database_name);
```

Query performance monitoring and profiling are essential for identifying performance bottlenecks, analyzing query execution plans, and optimizing database operations. Database administrators can use query profiling tools and utilities to capture and analyze query execution statistics, identify slow-running queries, and pinpoint areas for optimization. By monitoring query performance metrics, administrators can identify opportunities for improvement, optimize database configurations, and ensure optimal system performance and responsiveness.

bashCopy code

```
# Example command to enable query profiling in PostgreSQL SET profiling = 1;
```

In summary, query optimization strategies are essential for improving the performance and efficiency of database queries, ensuring fast and responsive data retrieval in database-driven applications. By employing techniques such as indexing, table partitioning, query rewriting, query hints, database configuration tuning, query caching, sharding, replication, and query performance monitoring, administrators and developers can optimize query performance, minimize resource utilization, and deliver a better user experience. Query optimization should be an ongoing process, with administrators continuously analyzing query performance, identifying areas for improvement, and implementing optimizations to ensure optimal database performance and user satisfaction.

Chapter 8: Multithreading and Concurrency: Utilizing Threads and Executors

Multithreading Fundamentals are essential for developers seeking to build responsive and efficient software applications capable of handling concurrent tasks and maximizing system resources. Multithreading enables applications to execute multiple threads of execution concurrently, allowing tasks to run in parallel and take advantage of modern multi-core processors. By understanding multithreading fundamentals, developers can design and implement applications that leverage concurrency to improve performance, responsiveness, and scalability.

One of the fundamental concepts in multithreading is a thread, which represents a single sequence of execution within a process. Threads allow applications to perform multiple tasks simultaneously by dividing the workload into smaller units of execution that can run concurrently. Threads share the same memory space and resources within a process, allowing them to communicate and synchronize their activities effectively. Creating and managing threads is essential for building multithreaded applications capable of leveraging concurrency to perform tasks more efficiently.

bashCopy code

```
# Example command to create a thread in Java Thread thread = new Thread(new Runnable() { public void run() { // Thread execution code } }); thread.start();
```

Concurrency control is another important aspect of multithreading fundamentals, ensuring that multiple threads can safely access and modify shared resources without causing data corruption or race conditions. Synchronization mechanisms such as locks, mutexes, and semaphores are used to coordinate access to shared resources and prevent concurrent access conflicts. By properly synchronizing access to critical sections of code, developers can ensure data integrity and avoid potential concurrency issues in multithreaded applications.

bashCopy code

```
# Example command to use a lock for synchronization in Python import threading lock = threading.Lock() def thread_function(): lock.acquire() try: # Critical section of code finally: lock.release()
```

Thread scheduling is another fundamental aspect of multithreading, determining the order in which threads are executed by the operating system's scheduler. Thread scheduling algorithms prioritize threads based on factors such as thread priority, time quantum, and CPU affinity, ensuring fair allocation of CPU resources among competing threads. Developers can influence thread scheduling behavior by adjusting thread priorities, setting CPU affinity masks, and implementing custom scheduling policies to optimize application performance and responsiveness.

bashCopy code

```
# Example command to set thread priority in C# Thread.CurrentThread.Priority = ThreadPriority.High;
```

Thread synchronization mechanisms such as locks and condition variables are essential for coordinating access to shared resources and managing thread interactions in multithreaded applications. Locks provide exclusive access to critical sections of code, ensuring that only one thread can execute the protected code at a time. Condition variables enable threads to wait for specific conditions to be satisfied before proceeding with execution, allowing for efficient inter-thread communication and synchronization.

bashCopy code

```
# Example command to use a condition variable in C++
#include <mutex> #include <condition_variable>
std::mutex mutex; std::condition_variable cond_var; void
thread_function() { std::unique_lock<std::mutex>
lock(mutex); cond_var.wait(lock); // Thread execution code
}
```

Thread safety is a critical consideration in multithreaded programming, ensuring that shared data structures and resources are accessed and modified safely by multiple threads. Thread-safe data structures and synchronization techniques such as locks, atomic operations, and thread-safe containers are used to prevent data corruption and race conditions in multithreaded applications. By designing thread-safe code and using appropriate synchronization mechanisms, developers can ensure data integrity and reliability in concurrent environments.

bashCopy code

```
# Example command to use a thread-safe container in C++
#include <mutex> #include <queue> std::mutex mutex;
std::queue<int> data_queue; void push_data(int value) {
std::lock_guard<std::mutex> lock(mutex);
data_queue.push(value); }
```

Deadlock and livelock are common concurrency issues that can occur in multithreaded applications, leading to system hangs or performance degradation. Deadlock occurs when two or more threads are blocked indefinitely, waiting for each other to release resources they need to proceed with execution. Livelock occurs when threads are continuously blocked or unable to make progress, often due to excessive resource contention or improper synchronization. Avoiding deadlock and livelock requires careful design and implementation of multithreaded code, ensuring proper synchronization and resource management to prevent contention and deadlock scenarios.

bashCopy code

```
# Example command to avoid deadlock by acquiring locks in a consistent order std::unique_lock<std::mutex> lock1(mutex1, std::defer_lock); std::unique_lock<std::mutex> lock2(mutex2, std::defer_lock); std::lock(lock1, lock2);
```

Thread pools are a common concurrency pattern used to manage and reuse a fixed number of threads for executing tasks asynchronously in multithreaded applications. Thread pools help reduce the overhead of creating and destroying threads dynamically by maintaining a pool of pre-allocated threads that can be reused for executing multiple tasks concurrently. By using thread pools, developers can improve application performance, reduce resource consumption, and simplify thread management in multithreaded applications.

bashCopy code

```
# Example command to create a thread pool in Java using ThreadPoolExecutor ThreadPoolExecutor executor = new ThreadPoolExecutor( corePoolSize, maxPoolSize, keepAliveTime, TimeUnit.SECONDS, new LinkedBlockingQueue<Runnable>() ); executor.execute(task);
```

In summary, understanding multithreading fundamentals is essential for developing scalable, responsive, and efficient software applications capable of leveraging concurrency to maximize system resources and performance. By mastering concepts such as threads, concurrency control, thread scheduling, synchronization mechanisms, thread safety, deadlock/livelock prevention, and thread pools, developers can design and implement multithreaded applications that effectively utilize parallelism to improve responsiveness and scalability. Multithreading is a powerful tool for enhancing application performance and responsiveness, but it requires careful design, implementation, and testing to ensure correct behavior and avoid common concurrency pitfalls.

Concurrency Patterns and Best Practices are essential for developers designing and implementing multithreaded software applications, ensuring efficient utilization of system resources, and maximizing performance and scalability. Concurrency patterns provide reusable solutions to common challenges encountered in concurrent programming, offering guidance on how to design and structure multithreaded applications effectively. By understanding and applying concurrency patterns and best practices, developers can build robust, responsive, and scalable software systems capable of handling concurrent tasks efficiently.

One of the most widely used concurrency patterns is the Thread Pool pattern, which involves creating a pool of pre-allocated threads to execute tasks asynchronously. Thread pools help reduce the overhead of thread creation and destruction by reusing existing threads for executing multiple tasks concurrently. By maintaining a fixed number of threads in the pool and queuing incoming tasks for execution, developers can optimize resource utilization, improve application responsiveness, and simplify thread management.

bashCopy code

Example command to create a thread pool in Java using ExecutorService ExecutorService executor =

```
Executors.newFixedThreadPool(poolSize);
executor.submit(task);
```

The Producer-Consumer pattern is another common concurrency pattern used to coordinate the interaction between multiple threads producing and consuming data. In this pattern, one or more producer threads generate data and add it to a shared buffer, while one or more consumer threads retrieve and process the data from the buffer. By decoupling the production and consumption of data, developers can improve system responsiveness, avoid contention for shared resources, and balance the workload between producers and consumers.

bashCopy code

```
# Example command to implement the Producer-Consumer pattern in Java using BlockingQueue BlockingQueue<Integer> queue = new ArrayBlockingQueue<>(capacity); // Producer thread queue.put(data); // Consumer thread int data = queue.take();
```

The Reader-Writer pattern is used to manage concurrent access to shared resources where multiple threads may need to read or write data simultaneously. In this pattern, multiple reader threads can access the resource concurrently for reading operations, while exclusive access is granted to a single writer thread for writing operations. By allowing multiple readers to access the resource concurrently and ensuring exclusive access for writers, developers can maximize concurrency while maintaining data consistency and integrity.

bashCopy code

```
# Example command to implement the Reader-Writer pattern in C++ using shared_mutex std::shared_mutex
```

mutex; // Reader thread std::shared_lock<std::shared_mutex> lock(mutex); // Writer thread std::unique_lock<std::shared_mutex> lock(mutex);

The Monitor pattern is a synchronization mechanism used to protect shared resources and coordinate access to critical sections of code. In this pattern, a monitor object encapsulates shared data and provides synchronized methods for accessing and modifying the data. Only one thread can acquire the monitor's lock at a time, ensuring exclusive access to the monitor's methods and preventing concurrent access to shared resources. By encapsulating shared data and synchronization logic within a monitor object, developers can simplify concurrency management and ensure thread safety.

bashCopy code

Example command to implement the Monitor pattern in Java using synchronized methods public class Monitor { private int count; public synchronized void increment() { count++; } public synchronized int getCount() { return count; } }

The Barrier pattern is used to synchronize the execution of multiple threads by forcing them to wait at a barrier point until all threads have reached the same point. Once all threads have arrived at the barrier point, they are released simultaneously to continue execution. Barriers are commonly used in parallel algorithms and simulations to synchronize the progress of multiple threads and coordinate their activities. By synchronizing thread execution at barrier points, developers can ensure that all threads reach a consistent state before proceeding with the next phase of execution.

bashCopy code

```
# Example command to implement the Barrier pattern in C++ using std::barrier std::barrier barrier(num_threads); // Thread synchronization point barrier.arrive_and_wait();
```

The Future pattern is used to represent the result of an asynchronous computation or task that may not have completed yet. Futures provide a placeholder for the result of a computation, allowing other threads to continue execution while waiting for the result to become available. By using futures, developers can perform asynchronous computations and retrieve their results asynchronously, enabling parallelism and non-blocking execution in multithreaded applications.

bashCopy code

```
# Example command to use the Future pattern in C++ using std::future std::future<int> result = std::async(std::launch::async, []() { // Asynchronous computation return 42; }); // Wait for the result int value = result.get();
```

The Immutable Object pattern is used to create thread-safe objects whose state cannot be modified after construction. Immutable objects are inherently thread-safe because they cannot be modified once they are created, eliminating the need for synchronization and ensuring that their state remains consistent across multiple threads. By designing classes with immutable properties and enforcing immutability through proper encapsulation and initialization, developers can simplify concurrency management and avoid potential data corruption or race conditions.

bashCopy code

```
# Example command to implement the Immutable Object pattern in Java public class ImmutableObject { private final
```

int value; public ImmutableObject(int value) { this.value = value; } public int getValue() { return value; } }

In summary, concurrency patterns and best practices are essential for designing and implementing multithreaded software applications capable of maximizing performance, scalability, and responsiveness. By understanding and applying concurrency patterns such as Thread Pool, Producer-Consumer, Reader-Writer, Monitor, Barrier, Future, and Immutable Object, developers can effectively manage concurrent tasks, synchronize access to shared resources, and ensure thread safety in multithreaded environments. Concurrency patterns provide reusable solutions to common concurrency challenges, offering guidance on how to design concurrent systems that are robust, reliable, and efficient.

Chapter 9: Optimizing for Different Device Form Factors and Screen Sizes

Device Form Factor Analysis is crucial for developers and designers aiming to create user-friendly and adaptable software experiences across various devices and screen sizes. Understanding the diverse landscape of device form factors, including smartphones, tablets, laptops, desktops, wearables, and other emerging form factors, is essential for ensuring optimal usability, accessibility, and performance of software applications. By conducting form factor analysis, developers can gain insights into the characteristics, capabilities, and limitations of different devices, enabling them to tailor their applications to meet the needs and expectations of users across different platforms and devices.

Analyzing the form factor of a device involves assessing its physical dimensions, screen size, aspect ratio, resolution, input methods, and other hardware attributes that influence the user experience. Devices vary significantly in terms of size, shape, and functionality, ranging from pocket-sized smartphones with touchscreens to larger tablets with keyboards and stylus support. By understanding the form factor of each device, developers can design user interfaces that are optimized for the available screen real estate, input methods, and interaction paradigms, ensuring a seamless and intuitive user experience across different devices.

bashCopy code

```
# Example command to analyze device form factor using ADB (Android Debug Bridge) adb shell wm size adb shell wm density
```

Screen size and resolution are critical factors to consider when designing software applications for different devices. Screen sizes vary widely across devices, from small smartphone screens to large desktop monitors and multi-monitor setups. High-resolution displays, such as Retina displays on Apple devices, require developers to design high-quality graphics and user interfaces that look crisp and sharp on high-density screens. By optimizing layout and content for different screen sizes and resolutions, developers can ensure that their applications look and perform well on a variety of devices, regardless of screen size or pixel density.

bashCopy code

```
# Example command to analyze screen size and resolution using ADB (Android Debug Bridge) adb shell wm size adb shell wm density
```

Input methods and interaction paradigms also play a significant role in device form factor analysis. Devices may support various input methods, including touchscreens, keyboards, mice, trackpads, styluses, and voice commands, each of which has its own unique characteristics and usability considerations. Touchscreen devices, such as smartphones and tablets, offer intuitive touch-based interactions, while devices with keyboards and mice require different interaction paradigms and input mechanisms. By designing applications that support multiple input methods and interaction modes, developers can accommodate the diverse needs and preferences of users across different devices and form factors.

bashCopy code

```
# Example command to analyze input methods using ADB (Android Debug Bridge) adb shell dumpsys input
```

Device orientation and context are additional factors to consider in form factor analysis. Devices may support different screen orientations, including portrait and landscape modes, which can affect the layout and presentation of content in software applications. Furthermore, devices may have contextual attributes, such as location, motion, and environmental sensors, which can provide valuable input for enhancing the user experience. By leveraging device orientation and context information, developers can create adaptive and context-aware applications that respond intelligently to changes in device orientation, location, and user behavior.

bashCopy code

```
# Example command to analyze device orientation using ADB (Android Debug Bridge) adb shell dumpsys input
```

Accessibility and inclusivity considerations are essential aspects of device form factor analysis. Devices vary in terms of accessibility features, such as screen readers, magnification, color inversion, and alternative input methods, which are designed to accommodate users with disabilities and special needs. By designing applications with accessibility in mind, developers can ensure that their software is usable and accessible to a diverse range of users, regardless of their physical abilities or assistive technology requirements. Accessibility testing and evaluation are essential steps in form factor analysis, ensuring that applications meet the needs of all users and comply with accessibility standards and guidelines.

bashCopy code

```
# Example command to analyze accessibility features using ADB (Android Debug Bridge) adb shell settings get secure enabled_accessibility_services
```

Cross-platform compatibility is another important consideration in device form factor analysis. With the proliferation of devices running different operating systems, such as Android, iOS, Windows, macOS, and Linux, developers must ensure that their applications are compatible with a wide range of platforms and devices. Cross-platform development frameworks and tools, such as Xamarin, React Native, Flutter, and Electron, enable developers to create applications that run on multiple platforms with a single codebase, reducing development time and effort while maximizing reach and compatibility across different devices and form factors.

bashCopy code

```
# Example command to analyze cross-platform compatibility using platform-specific SDKs flutter devices react-native run-android react-native run-ios
```

In summary, device form factor analysis is essential for designing software applications that deliver a consistent and engaging user experience across different devices and platforms. By understanding the characteristics, capabilities, and limitations of various devices, developers can tailor their applications to meet the needs and expectations of users, ensuring optimal usability, accessibility, and performance across different form factors. Form factor analysis involves assessing factors such as screen size, resolution, input methods, orientation, context, accessibility features, and cross-platform compatibility, enabling developers to create adaptive and inclusive applications that work seamlessly across a diverse range of devices and environments.

Responsive Design and Optimization are crucial aspects of modern web development, ensuring that websites and web applications adapt seamlessly to various devices, screen sizes, and user contexts. Techniques for responsive design and optimization encompass a range of strategies aimed at delivering fast-loading, visually appealing, and user-friendly experiences across desktops, laptops, tablets, smartphones, and other devices. By employing these techniques, developers can create websites and web applications that provide consistent and engaging experiences to users, regardless of the device they are using.

One of the fundamental techniques for responsive design and optimization is the use of media queries in CSS (Cascading Style Sheets). Media queries allow developers to apply different styles to a webpage based on characteristics such as screen size, resolution, orientation, and device type. By defining breakpoints in the CSS code and specifying styles for each breakpoint, developers can create responsive layouts that adapt dynamically to changes in screen size and device characteristics.

bashCopy code

```
# Example command to define a media query in CSS @media screen and (max-width: 768px) { /* Styles for devices with a maximum width of 768 pixels */ }
```

Another important technique for responsive design and optimization is the use of flexible and fluid layouts. Flexible layouts use relative units such as percentages and ems to specify widths, heights, and margins, allowing content to adapt fluidly to changes in screen size and viewport dimensions. By designing layouts that scale proportionally with the viewport, developers can create websites and web applications that look good and function well on devices of all sizes.

bashCopy code

```
# Example command to specify a flexible layout in CSS using percentages .container { width: 80%; margin: 0 auto; }
```

Optimizing images and media assets is essential for responsive design and optimization, as large, high-resolution images can significantly impact page load times and performance, especially on mobile devices with limited bandwidth and processing power. Techniques such as image compression, lazy loading, and responsive images enable developers to deliver high-quality visuals without sacrificing performance or user experience.

bashCopy code

```
# Example command to compress images using ImageMagick
convert input.jpg -resize 800x600 -quality 80 output.jpg
```

Implementing a mobile-first approach is a best practice in responsive design and optimization, as it prioritizes the development of websites and web applications for mobile devices before scaling up to larger screens. By starting with a mobile-first mindset, developers can focus on delivering essential content and functionality to mobile users, ensuring a streamlined and optimized experience on smaller screens. As screen size increases, developers can progressively enhance the user experience with additional features and enhancements tailored to larger screens.

bashCopy code

```
# Example command to set viewport meta tag for mobile-first design in HTML <meta name="viewport" content="width=device-width, initial-scale=1">
```

Using CSS frameworks and libraries designed for responsive design can streamline the development process and help ensure consistency and compatibility across different devices and browsers. Popular CSS frameworks such as Bootstrap, Foundation, and Bulma provide pre-designed components, grids, and utilities for building responsive layouts and user interfaces quickly and efficiently. By leveraging these frameworks, developers can save time and effort while creating responsive websites and web applications that adhere to best practices and design principles.

bashCopy code

```
# Example command to install Bootstrap using npm (Node Package Manager) npm install bootstrap
```

Optimizing performance is a critical aspect of responsive design and optimization, as slow-loading websites and web applications can lead to poor user experiences, high bounce rates, and decreased engagement. Techniques such as code minification, resource concatenation, browser caching, and content delivery network (CDN) integration can help improve page load times and performance, ensuring that websites and web applications load quickly and respond smoothly on all devices.

bashCopy code

```
# Example command to concatenate and minify CSS files using Grunt grunt cssmin
```

Implementing responsive typography is essential for ensuring readability and accessibility across different devices and screen sizes. Techniques such as fluid typography, viewport units, and modular scale enable developers to create typography that scales proportionally with the viewport, ensuring optimal legibility and readability on all devices. By using responsive typography techniques, developers can enhance the visual appeal and usability of their websites and web applications across a wide range of devices and screen sizes.

bashCopy code

```
# Example command to specify responsive typography using viewport units in CSS body { font-size: calc(16px + 0.5vw); }
```

In summary, techniques for responsive design and optimization are essential for creating websites and web applications that deliver consistent, engaging, and user-friendly experiences across different devices and screen sizes. By employing techniques such as media queries, flexible layouts, image optimization, mobile-first design, CSS frameworks, performance optimization, responsive typography, and more, developers can create responsive and optimized websites and web applications that meet the needs and expectations of users on desktops, laptops, tablets, smartphones, and other devices. Responsive design and optimization techniques enable developers to adapt to the ever-changing landscape of web development and ensure that their creations remain relevant and accessible to users across various platforms and contexts.

Chapter 10: Continuous Integration and Automated Testing for Performance Assurance

Continuous Integration (CI) Setup for Performance Testing is crucial for ensuring that software applications meet performance requirements consistently throughout the development lifecycle. Performance testing is an essential aspect of software development, as it helps identify and address performance bottlenecks, scalability issues, and resource constraints early in the development process. By integrating performance testing into the CI pipeline, developers can detect performance regressions, monitor performance trends, and validate performance improvements automatically with each code change. Setting up continuous integration for performance testing involves configuring CI tools, integrating performance testing tools, defining performance test scenarios, executing performance tests automatically, and analyzing performance test results as part of the CI workflow.

One of the first steps in setting up continuous integration for performance testing is to choose a CI tool that supports performance testing integration. Popular CI tools such as Jenkins, Travis CI, CircleCI, and GitLab CI/CD provide support for integrating performance testing tools and executing performance tests as part of the CI pipeline. By installing and configuring the chosen CI tool, developers can establish a CI environment that automates the execution of performance tests and provides visibility into performance metrics and trends over time.

bashCopy code

Example command to install Jenkins using Docker docker run -d -p 8080:8080 jenkins/jenkins:lts

Once the CI tool is set up, the next step is to integrate performance testing tools into the CI pipeline. Performance testing tools such as Apache JMeter, Gatling, Locust, and k6 are commonly used for load testing, stress testing, and performance monitoring of software applications. By integrating these tools into the CI pipeline, developers can automate the execution of performance tests and analyze performance metrics in real-time as part of the CI workflow.

bashCopy code

Example command to install Apache JMeter using Homebrew (macOS) brew install jmeter

After integrating performance testing tools into the CI pipeline, developers need to define performance test scenarios that simulate real-world usage patterns and workload conditions. Performance test scenarios should include a combination of load tests, stress tests, endurance tests, and spike tests to evaluate different aspects of application performance under various conditions. By defining comprehensive performance test scenarios, developers can identify performance bottlenecks, assess system scalability, and validate performance improvements with each code change.

bashCopy code

Example command to create a performance test scenario in Apache JMeter jmeter -n -t testplan.jmx -l results.jtl

With performance test scenarios defined, developers can automate the execution of performance tests as part of the CI pipeline. By configuring the CI tool to trigger performance tests automatically on code changes, developers can ensure that performance testing is performed consistently and systematically throughout the development lifecycle.

Automated performance testing enables developers to detect performance regressions early, prevent performance issues from reaching production, and validate performance improvements with each code change.

bashCopy code

```
# Example command to execute performance tests in Jenkins pipeline pipeline { agent any stages { stage('Performance Test') { steps { sh 'jmeter -n -t testplan.jmx -l results.jtl' } } } }
```

Once performance tests are executed automatically, developers need to analyze performance test results to identify performance issues, trends, and improvements. Performance test results typically include metrics such as response time, throughput, error rate, CPU utilization, memory consumption, and network latency, which can be analyzed to assess application performance and scalability. By analyzing performance test results as part of the CI workflow, developers can gain insights into application performance, prioritize performance improvements, and optimize system resources effectively.

bashCopy code

```
# Example command to analyze performance test results using Apache JMeter jmeter -g results.jtl -o dashboard
```

Continuous integration for performance testing enables developers to detect and address performance issues early in the development process, ensuring that software applications meet performance requirements and user expectations consistently. By integrating performance testing into the CI pipeline, developers can automate the execution of performance tests, monitor performance trends, and validate performance improvements automatically with each code change. Continuous integration for performance testing promotes a proactive approach to performance management, enabling developers to deliver high-performance, scalable, and reliable software applications that meet the needs of users and stakeholders.

Automated Testing Strategies for Performance Assurance are critical components of the software development lifecycle, ensuring that applications meet performance requirements consistently and reliably. Performance assurance involves the systematic testing and validation of software applications to ensure optimal performance, scalability, and reliability under various workload conditions. Automated testing strategies for performance assurance encompass a range of techniques and tools aimed at automating the execution of performance tests, analyzing performance metrics, detecting performance regressions, and optimizing application performance throughout the development process. By adopting automated testing strategies for performance assurance, organizations can identify and address performance issues early, mitigate risks, and deliver high-performance software applications that meet the needs and expectations of users.

One of the key automated testing strategies for performance assurance is the use of load testing tools to simulate realistic user traffic and workload conditions. Load testing tools such as Apache JMeter, Gatling, Locust, and k6 enable developers to generate virtual user traffic, measure application response times, and assess system performance under various load levels. By automating the execution of load tests, developers can identify performance bottlenecks, assess system scalability, and validate performance improvements systematically throughout the development lifecycle.

bashCopy code

```bash
# Example command to execute a load test using Apache JMeter
jmeter -n -t testplan.jmx -l results.jtl
```

Another important automated testing strategy for performance assurance is the use of stress testing tools to evaluate application resilience and stability under extreme workload conditions. Stress testing tools such as Apache JMeter, Gatling, and Siege enable developers to simulate high levels of concurrent user traffic, resource utilization, and system stress to assess application performance under peak load scenarios. By automating the execution of stress tests, developers can identify performance limitations, assess system robustness, and optimize application performance under heavy load conditions.

bashCopy code

```bash
# Example command to execute a stress test using Gatling
gatling.sh -s MySimulation
```

Automated monitoring and profiling tools are essential for performance assurance, enabling developers to monitor application performance in real-time, identify performance bottlenecks, and analyze performance metrics systematically. Monitoring and profiling tools such as New Relic, Datadog, AppDynamics, and Prometheus provide insights into application performance, resource utilization, and system health, enabling developers to diagnose performance issues, optimize system resources, and improve application performance proactively.

bashCopy code

```bash
# Example command to monitor application performance using New Relic CLI
newrelic monitor -a my-application
```

Continuous integration (CI) and continuous delivery (CD) pipelines play a crucial role in automated testing strategies for performance assurance, enabling developers to automate the execution of performance tests, analyze performance metrics, and validate performance improvements with each code change. By integrating performance testing into the CI/CD pipeline, developers can detect performance regressions early, prevent performance issues from reaching production, and ensure that software applications meet performance requirements consistently throughout the development lifecycle.

bashCopy code

```
# Example command to configure a performance test stage in a Jenkins pipeline pipeline { agent any stages { stage('Performance Test') { steps { sh 'jmeter -n -t testplan.jmx -l results.jtl' } } } }
```

Automated anomaly detection and alerting mechanisms are essential for performance assurance, enabling developers to detect and respond to performance issues in real-time. Anomaly detection tools such as Prometheus, Grafana, and Nagios monitor application performance metrics, detect abnormal behavior, and trigger alerts or notifications when performance deviations occur. By automating anomaly detection and alerting, developers can identify performance issues promptly, investigate root causes, and mitigate risks before they impact users or business operations.

bashCopy code

```
# Example command to configure alerting rules in Prometheus alerting: rules: - alert: HighResponseTime expr: http_response_time_seconds > 1 for: 5m labels: severity: critical annotations: summary: "High response time detected" description: "The response time of the application is higher than expected."
```

Automated regression testing is essential for performance assurance, enabling developers to validate performance improvements and prevent performance regressions with each code change. Regression testing tools such as Apache JMeter, Gatling, and Selenium enable developers to automate the execution of performance tests, compare performance metrics between test runs, and detect performance regressions early. By integrating regression testing into the CI/CD pipeline, developers can ensure that performance improvements are validated systematically and reliably throughout the development lifecycle.

bashCopy code

```
# Example command to execute regression tests using Selenium WebDriver mvn test
```

In summary, automated testing strategies for performance assurance are essential for ensuring that software applications meet performance requirements consistently and reliably. By adopting automated testing strategies, organizations can identify and address performance issues early, optimize application performance, and deliver high-quality software applications that meet the needs and expectations of users. Automated testing strategies for performance assurance encompass techniques such as load testing, stress testing, monitoring, profiling, continuous integration, anomaly detection, alerting, and regression testing, enabling developers to validate performance improvements systematically and mitigate risks throughout the development lifecycle.

BOOK 4

ANDROID STUDIO PRO

ADVANCED TOOLS AND TIPS FOR POWER USERS

ROB BOTWRIGHT

Chapter 1: Advanced Debugging Techniques with Android Studio

Debugging with breakpoints and watchpoints is a fundamental aspect of software development, enabling developers to identify and resolve issues in their code efficiently. Breakpoints are markers placed in the code that pause program execution when reached, allowing developers to inspect variables, evaluate expressions, and step through code one line at a time. Watchpoints, on the other hand, are breakpoints set on variables, which pause execution when the value of the variable changes, providing insight into how data changes during runtime. By utilizing breakpoints and watchpoints effectively, developers can diagnose bugs, trace program flow, and understand the behavior of their code more deeply.

Setting breakpoints is a common debugging technique used by developers to pause program execution at specific points in the code. Most integrated development environments (IDEs) and debugging tools provide features to set breakpoints easily. For example, in Visual Studio Code, developers can set breakpoints by clicking on the line number in the code editor, or by pressing **F9** while the cursor is on the desired line.

bashCopy code

```
# Example command to set a breakpoint in Visual Studio Code F9
```

Once breakpoints are set, developers can run their code in debug mode, causing the program execution to pause when it reaches the breakpoints. At this point, developers can inspect the state of the program, including variable values, call stack, and other runtime information. They can also step through the code line by line, using commands such as "Step Over" to execute the current line and move to the next, or "Step Into" to enter function calls and trace their execution.

bashCopy code

```
# Example command to step over in Visual Studio Code
F10
```

Watchpoints are particularly useful for monitoring the value of specific variables during program execution. By setting watchpoints on variables, developers can pause execution whenever the value of the variable changes, allowing them to analyze how data evolves over time. This can be invaluable for identifying subtle bugs or understanding complex program behavior.

bashCopy code

```
# Example command to set a watchpoint in Visual Studio
Code watch variable_name
```

When a watchpoint is triggered, developers can inspect the current value of the variable and track how it changes as the program continues to execute. This can help pinpoint exactly when and where a variable's value is modified, making it easier to diagnose and fix bugs related to incorrect data manipulation.

In addition to traditional breakpoints and watchpoints, some debugging tools offer advanced features such as conditional breakpoints and hit counts. Conditional breakpoints allow developers to specify conditions under which the breakpoint should be triggered, enabling more fine-grained control over when program execution pauses. Hit counts, on the other hand, allow developers to specify how many times a breakpoint must be hit before pausing execution, which can be useful for debugging loops or repetitive code.

bashCopy code

```
# Example command to set a conditional breakpoint in Visual Studio Code breakpoint if variable_name == value
```

Another useful feature provided by some debugging tools is the ability to log messages or expressions during program execution. By inserting log statements at strategic points in the code, developers can track the flow of execution and monitor the values of variables without pausing the program. This can be helpful for debugging issues that occur during specific conditions or loops.

bashCopy code

```
# Example command to log a message in Visual Studio Code console.log("Debug message");
```

In summary, debugging with breakpoints and watchpoints is an essential skill for software developers, enabling them to identify and resolve issues in their code effectively. By setting breakpoints at critical points in the code and utilizing watchpoints to monitor variable values, developers can gain valuable insight into how their programs behave during runtime. With the help of modern debugging tools and features such as conditional breakpoints, hit counts, and logging, developers can streamline the debugging process and expedite the resolution of bugs, ultimately leading to more robust and reliable software applications.

Using advanced debugging features like conditional breakpoints enhances the efficiency and precision of debugging processes, providing developers with more control and insight into their code. Conditional breakpoints allow developers to specify conditions under which a breakpoint should be triggered, enabling them to pause program execution only when certain criteria are met. This capability is particularly useful when debugging complex codebases or when trying to isolate specific issues that occur under certain conditions. By leveraging conditional breakpoints effectively, developers can streamline the debugging process, reduce debugging time, and gain a deeper understanding of their code's behavior.

Setting up conditional breakpoints involves specifying conditions that must be met for the breakpoint to be triggered. Most integrated development environments (IDEs) and debugging tools provide intuitive interfaces for defining these conditions. For example, in Visual Studio Code, developers can set conditional breakpoints by right-clicking on a breakpoint and selecting "Edit Breakpoint." They can then enter the desired condition using a simple expression syntax, such as checking the value of a variable or evaluating a logical expression.

bashCopy code

```
# Example command to set a conditional breakpoint in Visual Studio Code breakpoint if variable_name == value
```

Once a conditional breakpoint is set, the debugger will pause program execution only when the specified condition evaluates to true. This allows developers to focus their debugging efforts on specific scenarios or code paths where issues are likely to occur, saving time and effort compared to traditional breakpoints that pause execution indiscriminately.

Conditional breakpoints can be particularly helpful when debugging code that is executed multiple times within a loop or an iterative process. By setting conditions that filter out irrelevant iterations, developers can quickly identify and diagnose issues without having to step through every iteration manually. This can significantly accelerate the debugging process, especially in cases where the code undergoes numerous iterations or loops.

bashCopy code

```
# Example command to set a conditional breakpoint within a loop in Visual Studio Code breakpoint if iteration_number == target_iteration
```

In addition to filtering breakpoints based on variable values, developers can also use conditional breakpoints to debug code based on more complex conditions, such as the state of the program or the outcome of a function call. For example, developers can set breakpoints that trigger only when certain exceptions are thrown, specific methods are called, or specific conditions are met within the code.

bashCopy code

```
# Example command to set a conditional breakpoint based on a function call in Visual Studio Code breakpoint if function_name() == desired_result
```

Conditional breakpoints are also valuable for debugging asynchronous code or event-driven applications, where traditional breakpoints may not be effective. By setting breakpoints that trigger only when specific events occur or specific asynchronous operations complete, developers can debug complex asynchronous code more effectively, without having to rely on manual inspection or logging.

bashCopy code

Example command to set a conditional breakpoint on an asynchronous event in Visual Studio Code breakpoint if event == desired_event

In summary, using advanced debugging features like conditional breakpoints can significantly improve the efficiency and effectiveness of the debugging process. By allowing developers to specify conditions under which breakpoints should be triggered, conditional breakpoints enable more targeted and focused debugging efforts, reducing the time and effort required to diagnose and resolve issues in the code. Whether debugging loops, asynchronous code, or complex conditional logic, conditional breakpoints provide developers with the flexibility and control they need to debug their code with precision and confidence.

Chapter 2: Profiling and Performance Monitoring Tools

Utilizing Android Profiler for performance analysis is a fundamental aspect of Android app development, providing developers with powerful tools and insights to optimize their applications for performance, responsiveness, and resource efficiency. The Android Profiler is an integrated toolset available in Android Studio that allows developers to monitor various aspects of their app's performance in real-time, including CPU, memory, network, and battery usage. By leveraging the capabilities of the Android Profiler, developers can identify performance bottlenecks, diagnose performance issues, and optimize their apps to deliver a smooth and responsive user experience.

One of the key features of the Android Profiler is its ability to monitor CPU usage during app execution. The CPU Profiler provides developers with detailed information about how their app utilizes the device's CPU resources, including CPU usage by thread, method, and component. By analyzing CPU usage patterns, developers can identify performance hotspots, inefficient algorithms, and CPU-intensive tasks that may be impacting app performance negatively.

bashCopy code

```
# Example command to open the CPU Profiler in Android Studio profile cpu
```

In addition to CPU usage, the Android Profiler also allows developers to monitor memory usage and track memory allocations in real-time. The Memory Profiler provides insights into how the app allocates and manages memory, including heap memory, native memory, and memory leaks. By monitoring memory usage and analyzing memory allocation patterns, developers can identify memory leaks, excessive memory consumption, and inefficient memory management practices that may lead to performance degradation or app crashes.

bashCopy code

```
# Example command to open the Memory Profiler in Android Studio profile memory
```

The Network Profiler is another essential tool provided by the Android Profiler, allowing developers to monitor network activity and analyze network performance metrics. With the Network Profiler, developers can view network requests, responses, and data transfer rates in real-time, helping them identify network-related performance issues, such as slow network requests, excessive data usage, or network timeouts. By optimizing network usage and reducing network latency, developers can enhance app responsiveness and improve the overall user experience.

bashCopy code

```
# Example command to open the Network Profiler in Android Studio profile network
```

Battery consumption is a critical aspect of app performance, particularly for mobile devices with limited battery life. The Energy Profiler in the Android Profiler allows developers to monitor battery usage and analyze power consumption patterns while the app is running. By identifying power-hungry app components, inefficient battery usage, and background processes that drain battery life, developers can optimize their apps to minimize energy consumption and prolong battery life, ensuring a better user experience and increased device longevity.

bashCopy code

```
# Example command to open the Energy Profiler in Android Studio profile energy
```

The Android Profiler also includes other useful tools and features, such as GPU Profiler for monitoring graphics rendering performance, System Trace for capturing detailed system-level performance data, and Custom Profilers for creating custom performance monitoring dashboards. These tools provide developers with comprehensive insights into various aspects of app performance, allowing them to diagnose performance issues effectively and optimize their apps for better performance, responsiveness, and efficiency.

bashCopy code

```
# Example command to open the GPU Profiler in Android Studio profile gpu
```

Integrating the Android Profiler into the development workflow is straightforward, as it is seamlessly integrated into Android Studio, the official IDE for Android app development. Developers can access the Android Profiler directly from Android Studio's toolbar or menu, allowing them to monitor app performance and analyze performance metrics effortlessly. By regularly profiling their apps during development and testing, developers can identify performance issues early, iterate on optimizations, and ensure that their apps deliver a smooth and responsive user experience across a wide range of devices and usage scenarios.

In summary, utilizing the Android Profiler for performance analysis is essential for optimizing Android apps for performance, responsiveness, and resource efficiency. By leveraging the various tools and features provided by the Android Profiler, developers can monitor CPU, memory, network, and battery usage in real-time, diagnose performance issues, and optimize their apps to deliver a superior user experience. With its seamless integration into Android Studio and comprehensive performance monitoring capabilities, the Android Profiler empowers developers to build high-quality Android apps that meet the performance expectations of users and stakeholders.

Monitoring app performance with tools like Systrace and Traceview is crucial for developers to ensure their applications run smoothly and efficiently on Android devices. These tools provide deep insights into various aspects of an app's performance, including CPU usage, thread activity, method execution times, and system-level interactions. By leveraging Systrace and Traceview effectively, developers can identify performance bottlenecks, diagnose issues, and optimize their apps for better responsiveness and user experience.
Systrace is a powerful performance profiling tool built into the Android platform, allowing developers to capture detailed system-level traces of their applications. It provides a comprehensive view of the system's behavior during app execution, including CPU scheduling, thread activity, interrupts, and system calls. Systrace captures data from multiple sources, including the kernel, user-space libraries, and application code, enabling developers to analyze performance across the entire system stack.
bashCopy code

```
# Example command to capture a Systrace trace on a connected Android device adb shell systrace
```

Once a Systrace trace is captured, developers can analyze it using the Systrace Viewer tool, which is part of the Android SDK. The Systrace Viewer provides a graphical representation of the trace data, allowing developers to visualize system activity over time and identify performance anomalies, such as CPU spikes, thread contention, or excessive system calls. By analyzing Systrace traces, developers can pinpoint performance issues at the system level and optimize their apps accordingly.

Traceview, on the other hand, is a profiling tool that focuses on method-level performance analysis within an application. It allows developers to capture method traces during app execution, providing insights into the execution times of individual methods and the call hierarchy within the application code. Traceview is particularly useful for identifying performance bottlenecks within specific code paths and optimizing the critical sections of an application.

bashCopy code

```
# Example command to capture a Traceview trace on a connected Android device adb shell am profile start com.example.myapp
```

bashCopy code

```
# Example command to stop capturing a Traceview trace
adb shell am profile stop
```

Once a Traceview trace is captured, developers can analyze it using the Traceview tool, which is also part of the Android SDK. Traceview displays method call stacks, execution times, and other performance metrics in a graphical interface, allowing developers to visualize the flow of execution within their application code and identify areas for optimization. By analyzing Traceview traces, developers can optimize method performance, reduce execution times, and improve the overall responsiveness of their apps.

Both Systrace and Traceview are invaluable tools for app performance monitoring and optimization, offering complementary insights into different aspects of an app's performance. While Systrace provides a system-wide view of performance, Traceview focuses on method-level analysis within the application code. By combining the insights from both tools, developers can gain a comprehensive understanding of their app's performance characteristics and make informed decisions to improve performance.

In addition to capturing traces directly from a connected Android device, developers can also integrate Systrace and Traceview into their build and testing processes using Gradle tasks or Android Studio's profiling tools. This allows developers to automate performance monitoring and analysis as part of their development workflow, ensuring that performance considerations are addressed early and consistently throughout the development lifecycle.

In summary, monitoring app performance with tools like Systrace and Traceview is essential for developers to identify performance issues, diagnose bottlenecks, and optimize their applications for better responsiveness and user experience. By capturing and analyzing traces at both the system and method levels, developers can gain deep insights into their app's performance characteristics and make data-driven decisions to improve performance. With their integration into the Android SDK and development tools, Systrace and Traceview empower developers to build high-performance Android apps that meet the expectations of users and stakeholders.

Chapter 3: Using Android Studio Templates and Code Snippets Effectively

Exploring and customizing Android Studio templates is an essential aspect of Android app development, allowing developers to streamline their workflow, enforce coding standards, and promote consistency across projects. Android Studio provides a variety of templates for creating new Android projects, activities, fragments, and other components, which serve as starting points for app development. By exploring and customizing these templates, developers can tailor them to their specific needs, incorporating best practices, libraries, and design patterns to accelerate development and improve code quality.

To explore Android Studio templates, developers can navigate to the "New Project" or "New" menu within Android Studio and select the desired template type. This opens a dialog that displays a list of available templates, organized by category, such as "Activity," "Fragment," "Service," and "Layout." Developers can browse through the templates, view their descriptions, and choose the one that best fits their requirements.

bashCopy code

```
# Example command to create a new project using a template in Android Studio File > New > New Project
```

Once a template is selected, developers can customize it to meet their specific needs. Android Studio provides several options for customizing templates, including modifying the code, adding or removing dependencies, and configuring project settings. Developers can also create their own custom templates or modify existing ones to suit their development workflow and preferences.

bashCopy code
Example command to create a new activity using a template in Android Studio File > New > Activity > Basic Activity

One common customization technique is to modify the default code generated by the template to incorporate project-specific requirements, such as application logic, user interface elements, and third-party libraries. Developers can edit the template files directly within Android Studio's code editor, making changes to the layout XML files, Java classes, and resource files as needed.

bashCopy code
Example command to open a template file for editing in Android Studio Navigate > Open File

Another customization option is to add or remove dependencies from the project's build.gradle file. Android Studio's Gradle integration makes it easy to manage project dependencies, allowing developers to include libraries, frameworks, and plugins with just a few lines of code. By adding relevant dependencies to the project, developers can leverage existing functionality and reduce development effort.

bashCopy code
Example command to add a dependency to the build.gradle file in Android Studio implementation 'com.example:library:1.0.0'

Developers can also customize project settings, such as package names, application IDs, and minimum SDK versions, to align with project requirements and conventions. Android Studio provides a graphical interface for configuring project settings, allowing developers to specify various options during project creation or modify them later as needed.

bashCopy code

```
# Example command to configure project settings in Android Studio File > Project Structure
```

For more advanced customization, developers can create their own custom templates or modify existing ones using Android Studio's template editor. The template editor provides a visual interface for designing templates, allowing developers to define placeholders, variables, and custom logic to generate code dynamically. By creating custom templates, developers can standardize project structure, enforce coding conventions, and promote best practices across their organization.

bashCopy code

```
# Example command to open the template editor in Android Studio Tools > Android > Android Studio Preferences > File and Code Templates
```

In summary, exploring and customizing Android Studio templates is a valuable skill for Android app developers, enabling them to streamline their workflow, enforce coding standards, and promote consistency across projects. By leveraging Android Studio's built-in templates, developers can accelerate development and improve code quality by starting with a solid foundation. Whether modifying default code, adding dependencies, or creating custom templates, developers can tailor Android Studio templates to their specific needs and preferences, empowering them to build high-quality Android apps efficiently and effectively.

Creating and utilizing custom code snippets for productivity is a practice embraced by many developers to expedite coding tasks, enforce coding standards, and improve overall efficiency. Code snippets are small, reusable pieces of code that can be inserted into a codebase with minimal effort, reducing the need to type repetitive or boilerplate code manually. By creating custom code snippets tailored to specific use cases, developers can automate common coding patterns, eliminate errors, and enhance their workflow.

In modern integrated development environments (IDEs) like Visual Studio Code, Sublime Text, and IntelliJ IDEA, creating custom code snippets is straightforward and highly customizable. These IDEs provide built-in functionality for defining and managing code snippets, allowing developers to create, edit, and organize snippets according to their preferences.

The process of creating custom code snippets typically involves defining a trigger keyword or abbreviation that expands into the corresponding code snippet when entered in the code editor. For example, in Visual Studio Code, developers can create custom snippets using the built-in snippet creation tool or by manually editing the "snippets.json" file.

bashCopy code

```
# Example command to create a new custom code snippet in Visual Studio Code File > Preferences > User Snippets > New Global Snippets file
```

Once a custom snippet is defined, developers can use it by typing the trigger keyword in the code editor and pressing the appropriate shortcut key or key combination to expand the snippet. This instantly inserts the predefined code snippet at the cursor position, saving time and effort compared to typing the code manually.

bashCopy code

```
# Example command to insert a custom code snippet in Visual Studio Code Type trigger_keyword and press Tab
```

Custom code snippets can be tailored to various use cases and programming languages, making them versatile tools for improving productivity across different projects and workflows. For example, developers can create snippets for commonly used code patterns, such as class definitions, function declarations, or error handling routines, and insert them into their codebase with a single keystroke.

Beyond basic code insertion, custom code snippets can also include placeholders, variables, and tab stops, allowing developers to customize snippet behavior and adapt it to specific contexts. Placeholders enable developers to define dynamic parts of the snippet that can be customized each time the snippet is inserted, such as variable names, method parameters, or placeholder text. By leveraging placeholders, developers can create more flexible and reusable snippets that adapt to different coding scenarios.

bashCopy code

```
# Example command to create a custom code snippet with placeholders in Visual Studio Code "Print Statement": { "prefix": "log", "body": [ "console.log('${1:message}')" ], "description": "Log message to console" }
```

In addition to individual code snippets, developers can organize and manage their snippets effectively using snippet libraries or packages provided by IDE extensions or plugins. These libraries often include a collection of curated snippets for common programming tasks, frameworks, or libraries, saving developers the time and effort of creating snippets from scratch.

bashCopy code

```
# Example command to install a snippet library extension in Visual Studio Code Extensions > Search for "snippet library" > Install
```

Furthermore, some IDEs support sharing and synchronizing custom code snippets across multiple development environments, enabling developers to maintain a consistent set of snippets across different machines or team members.

This synchronization can be achieved through built-in synchronization features, cloud-based storage services, or version control systems, ensuring that custom snippets are always up-to-date and accessible wherever developers work.

bashCopy code

```bash
# Example command to synchronize custom code snippets using a cloud-based service Settings > Sync > Enable Sync
```

In summary, creating and utilizing custom code snippets for productivity is a valuable practice for developers looking to streamline their workflow, reduce repetitive tasks, and enforce coding standards. By defining custom snippets tailored to specific use cases and programming languages, developers can automate common coding patterns, eliminate errors, and accelerate development. With support for placeholders, variables, and snippet libraries, custom code snippets offer a flexible and efficient way to enhance coding productivity and consistency across projects and teams.

Chapter 4: Customizing Your Development Environment with Plugins and Extensions

Installing and managing plugins in Android Studio is a fundamental aspect of customizing the development environment to meet specific requirements and enhance productivity. Android Studio provides a robust plugin ecosystem that extends its functionality with additional features, tools, and integrations, empowering developers to tailor their IDE to their workflow preferences and project needs.

The process of installing plugins in Android Studio is straightforward and can be done directly from the IDE's integrated Plugin Marketplace. Developers can access the Plugin Marketplace by navigating to the "Settings" menu, selecting "Plugins," and then clicking on the "Browse repositories" button. This opens a window where developers can search for available plugins, browse categories, and install plugins with a single click.

bashCopy code

```
# Example command to access the Plugin Marketplace in Android Studio File > Settings > Plugins > Browse repositories
```

Once in the Plugin Marketplace, developers can explore a wide range of plugins categorized by functionality, such as code editing, version control, testing, and UI design. Popular plugins include support for additional programming languages, integration with third-party libraries and frameworks, code analysis and refactoring tools, and productivity enhancements like code generation and automation.

bashCopy code

```
# Example command to search for a specific plugin in the Plugin Marketplace Search for "plugin_name"
```

To install a plugin, developers can simply select the desired plugin from the list, click the "Install" button, and follow the on-screen instructions to complete the installation process. Android Studio will download and install the plugin automatically, and prompt the developer to restart the IDE to apply the changes. Once installed, the plugin's functionality becomes available within Android Studio, typically accessible through new menu options, toolbar buttons, or context menu actions.

bashCopy code

```
# Example command to install a plugin from the Plugin Marketplace in Android Studio Click "Install" on the desired plugin and follow the prompts
```

In addition to browsing and installing plugins from the Plugin Marketplace, developers can also manage installed plugins directly within Android Studio. The "Plugins" settings page provides options to enable, disable, update, and uninstall plugins, allowing developers to customize their IDE's feature set and optimize performance by disabling unnecessary plugins.

bashCopy code

```
# Example command to manage installed plugins in Android Studio File > Settings > Plugins
```

From the "Plugins" settings page, developers can view a list of installed plugins, along with their current status, version, and provider. By selecting a plugin, developers can enable or disable it with a single click, effectively controlling which plugins are active and which are not. Additionally, developers can check for updates to installed plugins and install updates as they become available, ensuring that plugins stay up-to-date with the latest features and bug fixes.

bashCopy code

```
# Example command to check for updates to installed plugins in Android Studio Click "Check for updates" on the "Plugins" settings page
```

Furthermore, Android Studio supports the installation of plugins from external sources, such as third-party websites or custom plugin repositories. Developers can download plugin files (typically in .zip or .jar format) from these sources and install them manually using the "Install plugin from disk" option in the "Plugins" settings page. This allows developers to leverage plugins not available in the Plugin Marketplace or customize existing plugins to suit their specific needs.

bashCopy code

```
# Example command to install a plugin from a local file in Android Studio File > Settings > Plugins > Install plugin from disk
```

In summary, installing and managing plugins in Android Studio is essential for customizing the development environment and enhancing productivity. By leveraging the Plugin Marketplace, developers can browse, install, and update plugins with ease, extending Android Studio's functionality with additional features and tools. With options to enable, disable, and uninstall plugins, developers have full control over their IDE's feature set, ensuring a tailored development experience that meets their workflow requirements. Whether installing plugins from the Plugin Marketplace or external sources, Android Studio provides a flexible and customizable platform for developers to optimize their development workflow and build high-quality Android apps efficiently.

Customizing IDE settings for enhanced productivity is a crucial aspect of optimizing the development environment to suit individual preferences and workflow requirements. Modern integrated development environments (IDEs) like Visual Studio Code, IntelliJ IDEA, and Sublime Text offer a plethora of customization options that allow developers to tailor their environment to their liking, streamline their workflow, and boost efficiency.

The process of customizing IDE settings typically involves navigating through various configuration menus and dialogs to adjust preferences related to code formatting, syntax highlighting, keyboard shortcuts, code completion, and many other aspects of the development experience. These settings can significantly impact a developer's productivity by providing a comfortable and efficient working environment tailored to their needs.

In Visual Studio Code, for example, developers can customize settings by accessing the "Settings" menu through the gear icon in the lower-left corner of the window or by pressing "Ctrl +,". This opens the settings editor, where developers can modify both user-specific settings and workspace-specific settings, allowing for fine-grained customization at both the individual and project levels.

bashCopy code

```
# Example command to access settings in Visual Studio Code
File > Preferences > Settings
```

The settings editor in Visual Studio Code provides a searchable list of available settings, organized into categories such as "Editor," "Workbench," "Extensions," and "Languages." Developers can use the search bar to quickly find specific settings or browse through the categories to discover available options. Each setting can be customized by clicking the edit icon next to it and entering the desired value or selecting from a list of options.

bashCopy code

Example command to search for a specific setting in Visual Studio Code Search for "setting_name" in the settings editor

One common customization in Visual Studio Code is configuring keyboard shortcuts to streamline common tasks and speed up navigation within the editor. Visual Studio Code allows developers to define custom keybindings for commands, editor actions, and extensions, enabling them to create personalized shortcuts that align with their workflow and habits.

bashCopy code

Example command to configure keyboard shortcuts in Visual Studio Code File > Preferences > Keyboard Shortcuts

In addition to keyboard shortcuts, developers can customize the appearance and behavior of the editor in Visual Studio Code by adjusting settings related to themes, fonts, colors, and layout. Visual Studio Code supports a wide range of themes and extensions that allow developers to personalize the look and feel of the IDE to match their preferences and style.

bashCopy code

Example command to install a theme extension in Visual Studio Code Extensions > Search for "theme_name" > Install

Similarly, IntelliJ IDEA provides extensive customization options through its settings dialog, which can be accessed by selecting "File > Settings" or by pressing "Ctrl + Alt + S". The settings dialog in IntelliJ IDEA is organized into categories such as "Editor," "Version Control," "Build, Execution, Deployment," and "Languages & Frameworks," allowing developers to fine-tune various aspects of the IDE to suit their needs.

bashCopy code

```
# Example command to access settings in IntelliJ IDEA File > Settings
```

Within the settings dialog, developers can customize editor behavior, code style, inspections, and keymaps, among other options. IntelliJ IDEA also supports the installation of plugins and extensions to further extend its functionality and customize the development experience.

bashCopy code

```
# Example command to install a plugin in IntelliJ IDEA File > Settings > Plugins > Browse repositories
```

Sublime Text offers similar customization capabilities through its settings menus and configuration files. Developers can access Sublime Text settings by selecting "Preferences > Settings" or by pressing "Ctrl +,". Sublime Text settings are defined in JSON format and allow developers to adjust various aspects of the editor, including preferences, key bindings, syntax-specific settings, and UI themes.

bashCopy code

```
# Example command to access settings in Sublime Text Preferences > Settings
```

By customizing IDE settings, developers can create a personalized development environment that aligns with their workflow, preferences, and habits. Whether adjusting code formatting options, configuring keyboard shortcuts, or installing themes and extensions, IDE customization empowers developers to work more efficiently and effectively, ultimately enhancing productivity and enjoyment of the development process.

Chapter 5: Version Control and Collaboration with Git and GitHub

Setting up version control with Git in Android Studio is an essential step for managing project changes, collaborating with team members, and ensuring code stability and integrity throughout the development process. Git, a distributed version control system, provides powerful features for tracking changes, branching, merging, and reverting to previous states, making it the de facto standard for version control in software development.

The process of setting up version control with Git in Android Studio begins by initializing a Git repository within the project directory. This can be done using the Git command-line interface (CLI) or through the built-in version control features of Android Studio. To initialize a Git repository via the CLI, developers can navigate to the project directory in the terminal and use the "git init" command to create a new Git repository.

bashCopy code

```
# Example command to initialize a Git repository via the CLI
cd path/to/project/directory git init
```

Alternatively, developers can initialize a Git repository directly within Android Studio by selecting "VCS > Import into Version Control > Create Git Repository" from the main menu. This prompts Android Studio to initialize a Git repository in the project directory and display the version control status of files within the IDE.

bashCopy code

Example command to initialize a Git repository in Android Studio VCS > Import into Version Control > Create Git Repository

Once the Git repository is initialized, developers can begin tracking changes to their project files by staging them for commit. In Android Studio, developers can stage changes by selecting the files or directories they wish to include in the commit and choosing "VCS > Git > Add" from the main menu. This adds the selected files to the staging area, preparing them for the next commit.

bashCopy code

Example command to stage changes in Android Studio VCS > Git > Add

After staging changes, developers can commit them to the Git repository along with a descriptive commit message to document the changes made. In Android Studio, developers can commit changes by selecting "VCS > Commit" from the main menu, which opens the commit dialog where they can review the staged changes, enter a commit message, and commit the changes to the repository.

bashCopy code

Example command to commit changes in Android Studio VCS > Commit

Throughout the development process, developers can use Git branches to isolate new features, bug fixes, or experimental changes from the main codebase. Creating a new branch in Git can be done via the CLI using the "git checkout -b" command followed by the desired branch name, or through Android Studio by selecting "VCS > Git > Branches > New Branch" from the main menu and entering the branch name.

bashCopy code

Example command to create a new branch via the CLI git checkout -b new_branch_name

bashCopy code

Example command to create a new branch in Android Studio VCS > Git > Branches > New Branch

After creating a new branch, developers can switch between branches using the "git checkout" command in the CLI or by selecting the desired branch from the Git branch dropdown menu in Android Studio. This allows developers to work on multiple features or fixes concurrently without affecting the main codebase.

bashCopy code

Example command to switch branches via the CLI git checkout branch_name

In addition to creating and switching branches, developers can merge branches back into the main codebase once their changes are complete and tested. Merging branches in Git can be done via the CLI using the "git merge" command followed by the name of the branch to be merged, or through Android Studio by selecting "VCS > Git > Merge Changes" from the main menu and choosing the branch to merge.

bashCopy code

Example command to merge branches via the CLI git merge branch_name

bashCopy code

Example command to merge branches in Android Studio VCS > Git > Merge Changes

In summary, setting up version control with Git in Android Studio is a fundamental aspect of modern software development that provides developers with powerful tools for managing project changes, collaborating with team members, and ensuring code stability and integrity. By initializing a Git repository, staging and committing changes, creating and switching branches, and merging branches, developers can effectively manage project evolution and streamline the development process within Android Studio's integrated version control features.

Collaborating with teammates using GitHub integration is a fundamental aspect of modern software development workflows that enables seamless communication, coordination, and code sharing among team members. GitHub, a popular web-based platform built around the Git version control system, provides a robust set of features for hosting repositories, managing issues and pull requests, reviewing code changes, and facilitating collaboration within development teams.

The process of collaborating with teammates using GitHub integration typically begins with creating a new repository on GitHub to host the project's codebase. This can be done through the GitHub website by clicking on the "New" button in the repositories tab, entering a name and description for the repository, and choosing options such as visibility (public or private) and initializing the repository with a README file.

bashCopy code

```
# Example command to create a new repository on GitHub git init git add . git commit -m "Initial commit" git branch -M main git remote add origin <repository_url> git push -u origin main
```

Once the repository is created, team members can clone the repository to their local development environments using the "git clone" command followed by the repository's URL. This creates a local copy of the repository on the developer's machine, allowing them to make changes to the codebase and contribute to the project.

bashCopy code

Example command to clone a repository from GitHub git clone <repository_url>

After cloning the repository, team members can work on different features or bug fixes in parallel by creating branches for each task using the "git checkout -b" command followed by the branch name. This isolates their changes from the main codebase until they are ready to be reviewed and merged.

bashCopy code

Example command to create a new branch for a feature or bug fix git checkout -b feature_branch_name

As team members make changes to the codebase, they can commit their changes to their local branches using the "git commit" command with a descriptive commit message to document the changes made. This captures a snapshot of the codebase at a specific point in time and allows team members to track the history of changes.

bashCopy code

Example command to commit changes to a local branch git add . git commit -m "Descriptive commit message"

Once changes are committed to a local branch, team members can push their changes to the remote repository on GitHub using the "git push" command followed by the branch name. This uploads their changes to the repository, making them available for review and integration into the main codebase.

bashCopy code

Example command to push changes to a remote repository on GitHub git push origin feature_branch_name

To integrate changes from a feature branch into the main codebase, team members can create a pull request on GitHub. This allows them to propose their changes for review by other team members, discuss any feedback or concerns, and eventually merge their changes into the main branch once they are approved.

bashCopy code

Example command to create a pull request on GitHub git push origin feature_branch_name

Throughout the development process, team members can use GitHub's issue tracking and project management features to coordinate tasks, track bugs, and prioritize work. Issues can be created and assigned to team members, labeled with tags to categorize them, and linked to specific pull requests for better traceability.

bashCopy code

```
# Example command to create a new issue on GitHub git push origin feature_branch_name
```

In addition to code changes, team members can also collaborate on documentation, code reviews, and discussions using GitHub's pull request and comment features. Pull requests provide a structured way for team members to review and discuss changes, provide feedback, and ensure code quality before merging changes into the main codebase.

bashCopy code

```
# Example command to create a comment on a pull request on GitHub git push origin feature_branch_name
```

In summary, collaborating with teammates using GitHub integration is a vital aspect of modern software development workflows that enables efficient communication, coordination, and code sharing among team members. By leveraging GitHub's powerful features for hosting repositories, managing issues and pull requests, and facilitating code reviews and discussions, development teams can streamline their collaboration efforts and build high-quality software more effectively.

Chapter 6: Harnessing the Power of Gradle Build System for Complex Projects

Understanding Gradle build scripts and configurations is essential for Android developers to effectively manage and customize their projects' build process. Gradle, a powerful build automation tool, is widely used in Android development to automate tasks such as compiling source code, packaging resources, and generating APKs. By delving into Gradle build scripts and configurations, developers can tailor the build process to their project's specific requirements, optimize build performance, and integrate third-party libraries and dependencies seamlessly.

At the heart of every Gradle project lies the build.gradle file, which serves as the entry point for defining project settings, dependencies, and tasks. This file, typically located in the root directory of the project, is written in Groovy or Kotlin DSL and is divided into two main sections: the buildscript block and the main configuration block.

The buildscript block is where developers specify the build script dependencies and repositories required to compile and execute the build script itself. This includes defining the Gradle plugin dependencies necessary for tasks such as compiling Java or Kotlin code, packaging resources, and generating APKs. Dependencies are declared using the dependencies block within the buildscript block, and repositories are specified using the repositories block.

bashCopy code

Example command to declare dependencies in the buildscript block buildscript { repositories { google() jcenter()

} dependencies { classpath 'com.android.tools.build:gradle:4.2.0' } }

The main configuration block, on the other hand, is where developers define project-specific settings, dependencies, and tasks. This includes configuring the Android plugin, specifying project-wide properties, and declaring dependencies required for building the project. Dependencies are declared using the dependencies block within the main configuration block, and project properties are defined using the ext block.

bashCopy code

Example command to declare dependencies in the main configuration block android { compileSdkVersion 31 buildToolsVersion "31.0.0" defaultConfig { applicationId "com.example.myapp" minSdkVersion 21 targetSdkVersion 31 versionCode 1 versionName "1.0" } ... } dependencies { implementation 'androidx.appcompat:appcompat:1.4.0' implementation 'com.google.android.material:material:1.5.0' ... }

In addition to defining project settings and dependencies, Gradle build scripts also allow developers to define custom tasks to automate project-specific tasks. These tasks can be defined using the task block within the build.gradle file and can perform a wide range of actions, such as copying files, executing shell commands, or running tests.

bashCopy code

Example command to define a custom task in a Gradle build script task customTask { doLast { println 'Executing custom task...' // Perform custom actions here } }

Furthermore, Gradle build scripts support a variety of plugins that extend the functionality of the build system and provide additional features for tasks such as code quality checks, code coverage, and dependency management. These plugins can be applied to the project using the plugins block within the build.gradle file, and their configurations can be customized as needed.

bashCopy code

```
# Example command to apply a plugin in a Gradle build script
plugins { id 'com.github.ben-manes.versions' version '0.39.0' }
```

Moreover, Gradle build scripts also support the use of build flavors and product flavors to customize the build process for different variants of the application. Build flavors allow developers to create variations of the application that share the same codebase but have different configurations, such as different package names, resources, or dependencies.

bashCopy code

```
# Example command to define build flavors in a Gradle build script android { ... flavorDimensions 'version' productFlavors { free { dimension 'version' ... } paid { dimension 'version' ... } } }
```

Additionally, Gradle build scripts offer powerful dependency management capabilities, allowing developers to declare and manage project dependencies efficiently. Dependencies can be declared using the dependencies block within the build.gradle file, and they can be specified using various notation formats, such as group:name:version, fileTree, or project.

bashCopy code

```
# Example command to declare dependencies in a Gradle build script dependencies { implementation 'com.google.android.material:material:1.5.0' testImplementation 'junit:junit:4.13.2' ... }
```

In summary, understanding Gradle build scripts and configurations is crucial for Android developers to effectively manage and customize their projects' build process. By mastering Gradle's syntax, features, and capabilities, developers can optimize build performance, integrate third-party libraries seamlessly, and automate project-specific tasks, ultimately streamlining the development workflow and improving productivity.

Optimizing build performance and managing dependencies are critical tasks in software development, particularly in Android development, where large codebases and complex dependency graphs can significantly impact build times. Gradle, the build automation tool widely used in Android projects, offers various techniques and strategies to improve build performance and streamline dependency management.

One of the primary approaches to optimizing build performance is by leveraging Gradle's build cache feature. The build cache stores task outputs from previous builds, allowing Gradle to reuse them in subsequent builds instead of re-executing the tasks. This can dramatically reduce build times, especially for tasks that are time-consuming or resource-intensive.

bashCopy code

```
# Example command to enable the build cache in a Gradle build script android { buildCache { local {} remote(HttpBuildCache) { url = 'http://localhost:8080/cache/' } } }
```

Another technique for optimizing build performance is by enabling incremental builds. Incremental builds only rebuild the parts of the project that have changed since the last build, rather than rebuilding the entire project from scratch.

This can significantly reduce build times, especially for large projects with many source files.

bashCopy code

```
# Example command to enable incremental builds in a Gradle build script android { compileOptions { incremental true } }
```

Additionally, developers can parallelize build tasks to further improve build performance. By running multiple tasks concurrently, Gradle can make better use of available CPU cores and resources, resulting in faster build times. Parallelization can be configured at both the task level and the project level in the Gradle build script.

bashCopy code

```
# Example command to configure parallel execution of tasks in a Gradle build script android { tasks.withType(JavaCompile) { options.compilerArgs << "-Xmaxerrs" << "10000" } }
```

Managing dependencies is another critical aspect of optimizing build performance in Android projects. Gradle provides several mechanisms for dependency management, including declaring dependencies in the build.gradle file, using dependency configurations, and resolving dependencies from remote repositories.

bashCopy code

```
# Example command to declare dependencies in a Gradle build script dependencies { implementation 'com.google.android.material:material:1.5.0' testImplementation 'junit:junit:4.13.2' ... }
```

To ensure efficient dependency resolution and minimize build times, developers can configure dependency caching. Dependency caching stores downloaded dependencies locally, allowing Gradle to reuse them in subsequent builds instead of re-downloading them from remote repositories. This can significantly reduce build times, especially in projects with large dependency trees.

bashCopy code

```
# Example command to enable dependency caching in a Gradle build script dependencies { implementation 'com.google.android.material:material:1.5.0'
testImplementation 'junit:junit:4.13.2' ... }
```

Moreover, developers can optimize dependency configurations to reduce the number of dependencies included in the project. This can involve excluding unnecessary transitive dependencies, splitting dependencies into smaller modules, or using lighter-weight alternatives where possible. By minimizing the number of dependencies, developers can reduce build times and project complexity.

bashCopy code

```
# Example command to exclude transitive dependencies in a Gradle build script dependencies {
implementation( 'com.android.support:appcompat-
v7:28.0.0' ) { exclude group: 'com.android.support', module:
'support-annotations' } }
```

In summary, optimizing build performance and managing dependencies are crucial tasks in Android development that can significantly impact project productivity and efficiency. By leveraging Gradle's features and techniques for build caching, incremental builds, parallel execution, and dependency management, developers can streamline the build process, reduce build times, and deliver high-quality software more efficiently.

Chapter 7: Advanced Testing Strategies: Unit Testing, UI Testing, and Espresso

Writing effective unit tests for Android apps is essential for ensuring code quality, identifying bugs early in the development process, and facilitating code maintenance and refactoring. Unit testing involves testing individual units or components of the application in isolation to verify their behavior and functionality. Android developers can use various testing frameworks and techniques to write comprehensive unit tests that cover different aspects of the application's functionality and behavior.

JUnit is the most commonly used testing framework for writing unit tests in Android applications. It provides annotations and assertions for writing tests and running them within the Android environment. By using JUnit, developers can write simple and expressive tests that validate the behavior of individual classes and methods in the application.

bashCopy code

```
# Example command to write a JUnit test in Android import org.junit.Test; import static org.junit.Assert.assertEquals; public class ExampleUnitTest { @Test public void addition_isCorrect() { assertEquals(4, 2 + 2); } }
```

In addition to JUnit, Android developers can leverage the Android Testing Support Library, which provides additional testing utilities and features specifically designed for Android applications. This library includes classes and annotations for writing tests that interact with the Android framework components, such as activities, fragments, and views.

bashCopy code

Example command to write an Android unit test using Android Testing Support Library import androidx.test.ext.junit.runners.AndroidJUnit4; import androidx.test.platform.app.InstrumentationRegistry; import androidx.test.filters.SmallTest; import org.junit.Test; import org.junit.runner.RunWith; import static org.junit.Assert.assertEquals;
@RunWith(AndroidJUnit4.class) @SmallTest public class ExampleInstrumentedTest { @Test public void useAppContext() { Context appContext = InstrumentationRegistry.getInstrumentation().getTargetContext(); assertEquals("com.example.myapp", appContext.getPackageName()); } }

When writing unit tests for Android apps, it's essential to follow best practices to ensure the effectiveness and reliability of the tests. One best practice is to write tests that are independent and isolated from each other, meaning that the outcome of one test should not depend on the state or outcome of another test. This helps to identify and isolate failures more easily and ensures that tests can be run in any order without affecting their results.

Another best practice is to use mock objects and dependency injection to isolate the unit under test from its dependencies. This allows developers to control the behavior of dependencies and focus on testing the specific functionality of the unit under test. Mockito is a popular mocking framework for Java and Android applications that allows developers to create and configure mock objects for testing purposes.

bashCopy code

Example command to use Mockito for mocking dependencies in Android unit tests import static org.mockito.Mockito.*; import org.junit.Test; public class MyUnitTest { @Test public void testSomething() { // Create a mock object MyDependency mockDependency = mock(MyDependency.class); // Configure the mock object when(mockDependency.someMethod()).thenReturn("mocked result"); // Inject the mock object into the unit under test MyClass myClass = new MyClass(mockDependency); // Perform the test // Verify the behavior of the unit under test } }

Furthermore, developers should strive to achieve high code coverage with their unit tests to ensure that critical parts of the codebase are thoroughly tested. Code coverage metrics, such as statement coverage, branch coverage, and path coverage, can help developers assess the effectiveness of their tests and identify areas of the code that need additional testing.

Continuous integration (CI) and continuous deployment (CD) pipelines can automate the process of running unit tests and ensuring code quality throughout the development lifecycle. By integrating unit tests into the CI/CD pipeline, developers can catch bugs early, validate code changes, and ensure that the application remains stable and reliable across different environments and configurations.

In summary, writing effective unit tests for Android apps is essential for ensuring code quality, identifying bugs early, and facilitating code maintenance and refactoring. By following best practices, leveraging testing frameworks and utilities, and integrating unit tests into the development process, developers can create robust and reliable Android applications that meet the needs and expectations of users.

Implementing UI tests with Espresso for UI automation is crucial for ensuring the quality and reliability of Android applications. Espresso is a powerful testing framework provided by Google that allows developers to write concise and expressive UI tests to simulate user interactions and validate the behavior of the application's user interface. By automating UI tests with Espresso, developers can detect regressions, identify bugs, and ensure that the application meets the expected user experience.

bashCopy code

```
# Example command to add Espresso dependencies to an Android project androidTestImplementation 'androidx.test.espresso:espresso-core:3.4.0'
androidTestImplementation 'androidx.test.ext:junit:1.1.3'
```

Espresso provides a fluent and intuitive API for writing UI tests, allowing developers to interact with UI components such as buttons, text fields, and list items programmatically. Tests are written in a behavior-driven style, using methods like **onView()** to locate UI elements and **perform()** to simulate user actions such as clicks, text input, and scrolling.

javaCopy code

```
// Example Espresso test to validate login functionality @Test public void testLogin() { // Type text and then press the button.
onView(withId(R.id.username_edit_text)).perform(typeText ("username" ));
onView(withId(R.id.password_edit_text)).perform(typeText( "password" ));
onView(withId(R.id.login_button)).perform(click()); // Check that the text was changed.
```

onView(withId(R.id.login_status_text)).check(matches(withText("Login successful"))); }

One of the key features of Espresso is its synchronization mechanism, which ensures that UI interactions and assertions are performed at the appropriate time during the test execution. Espresso automatically waits for the UI to become idle before performing actions or assertions, ensuring that tests are executed reliably and consistently across different devices and conditions.

Espresso also provides powerful matchers and assertions for validating the state and properties of UI elements. Developers can use matchers like **withId()**, **withText()**, and **isDisplayed()** to locate and verify the presence of UI components, while assertions like **matches()** and **doesNotExist()** can be used to verify the expected behavior of UI elements.

javaCopy code

```
// Example Espresso test to verify the presence of a button @Test public void testButtonPresence() { // Check if the button with the specified text is displayed onView(withText( "Submit" )).check(matches(isDisplayed()));
}
```

Moreover, Espresso supports advanced UI testing scenarios such as testing RecyclerViews, ViewPager, and navigation components. Developers can use additional Espresso APIs like **RecyclerViewActions** and **ViewPagerActions** to perform complex interactions such as scrolling, swiping, and selecting items in RecyclerViews and ViewPagers.

javaCopy code

```
// Example Espresso test to scroll RecyclerView to a specific item @Test public void testScrollToItem() { // Scroll RecyclerView to a specific item
```

onView(withId(R.id.recycler_view)).perform(RecyclerViewActions.scrollToPosition(10)); // Check if the item at position 10 is displayed onView(withText("Item 10")).check(matches(isDisplayed())); }

To maximize the effectiveness of UI tests with Espresso, developers should follow best practices such as creating small, focused tests that cover specific UI features or workflows, using meaningful test names and assertions, and minimizing dependencies on external factors such as network or device state.

Integrating UI tests with continuous integration (CI) pipelines is also essential for automating test execution and ensuring that UI tests are run consistently as part of the development process. Developers can use CI services like Jenkins, GitLab CI, or GitHub Actions to trigger UI tests automatically whenever changes are made to the codebase.

In summary, implementing UI tests with Espresso for UI automation is essential for ensuring the quality and reliability of Android applications. By leveraging Espresso's intuitive API, synchronization mechanism, and advanced testing capabilities, developers can write comprehensive UI tests that simulate user interactions, validate UI behavior, and identify issues early in the development lifecycle.

Chapter 8: Implementing Continuous Integration and Delivery Pipelines

Setting up continuous integration and continuous deployment (CI/CD) pipelines with tools like Jenkins or GitLab CI is essential for automating the software development lifecycle, streamlining the process of building, testing, and deploying applications, and ensuring consistent and reliable releases. These CI/CD pipelines enable developers to automate repetitive tasks, detect and fix issues early in the development process, and deliver high-quality software faster and more efficiently.

To set up a CI/CD pipeline with Jenkins, the first step is to install and configure Jenkins on a server or a cloud platform. Jenkins can be installed using various methods, including package managers like apt, yum, or brew, or by downloading and running the Jenkins war file directly.

bashCopy code

```
# Example command to install Jenkins using apt package manager sudo apt-get update sudo apt-get install jenkins
```

Once Jenkins is installed, it can be accessed via a web browser, and the initial setup wizard guides users through the process of configuring Jenkins and installing necessary plugins. Plugins are used to extend Jenkins' functionality and support features such as version control integration, build triggers, and reporting.

bashCopy code

```
# Example command to install Jenkins plugins using the Jenkins web interface Manage Jenkins > Manage Plugins > Available > [Select desired plugins] > Install
```

After configuring Jenkins, the next step is to create a Jenkins pipeline, which defines the stages and steps of the CI/CD process. A Jenkins pipeline is typically defined using a Jenkinsfile, which is written in Groovy syntax and stored alongside the project's source code in version control.

groovyCopy code

```
// Example Jenkinsfile defining a simple CI/CD pipeline
pipeline { agent any stages { stage('Build') { steps { sh 'mvn
clean package' } } stage('Test') { steps { sh 'mvn test' } }
stage('Deploy') { steps { sh 'ansible-playbook deploy.yml' } } }
}
```

In this example, the Jenkins pipeline consists of three stages: Build, Test, and Deploy. Each stage contains one or more steps, which are executed sequentially. The steps typically include commands to build the application, run tests, and deploy the application to a target environment.

Alternatively, GitLab CI provides built-in CI/CD capabilities integrated into GitLab's version control platform. To set up a CI/CD pipeline with GitLab CI, developers need to create a .gitlab-ci.yml file in the root directory of the project repository, which defines the pipeline configuration using YAML syntax.

yamlCopy code

```
# Example .gitlab-ci.yml file defining a CI/CD pipeline in
GitLab CI stages: - build - test - deploy build: stage:
build script: - mvn clean package test: stage: test script:
- mvn test deploy: stage: deploy script: - ansible-
playbook deploy.yml
```

Similar to Jenkins, the GitLab CI pipeline consists of stages and jobs, where each job contains a script to be executed. The pipeline configuration is stored in the .gitlab-ci.yml file, and changes to this file trigger the pipeline to run automatically.

Once the CI/CD pipeline is set up, developers can commit changes to the version control repository, triggering the pipeline to execute the defined stages and steps. The pipeline automates tasks such as building the application, running tests, and deploying the application to production or staging environments.
In addition to automation, CI/CD pipelines provide visibility into the software development process through detailed logs and reports, allowing developers to track the progress of builds and deployments, analyze test results, and troubleshoot issues as they arise.
Overall, setting up CI/CD pipelines with tools like Jenkins or GitLab CI is essential for automating and streamlining the software development lifecycle, enabling faster delivery of high-quality software and improving collaboration and visibility among development teams.

Automating app deployment and testing processes is essential for modern software development workflows, enabling faster releases, increased reliability, and improved overall efficiency. Automation streamlines repetitive tasks, reduces human error, and accelerates the feedback loop, ultimately leading to higher-quality software delivered more quickly to end-users.
One of the key aspects of automating app deployment and testing processes is the use of Continuous Integration/Continuous Deployment (CI/CD) pipelines. These pipelines automate the steps involved in building, testing, and deploying applications, ensuring that changes to the codebase are quickly and reliably integrated into the production environment.
bashCopy code

Example command to trigger a CI/CD pipeline git push origin main

CI/CD pipelines typically consist of several stages, including building the application, running unit tests, performing integration tests, and deploying the application to various environments. Each stage is comprised of one or more automated tasks or scripts that are executed sequentially.

For example, in a typical CI/CD pipeline, the first stage involves compiling the application code, packaging it into a deployable artifact, and storing it in a repository or artifact registry.

bashCopy code

```
# Example command to build and package the application
./gradlew clean build
```

Following the build stage, the next stage in the pipeline typically involves running automated tests to validate the functionality and performance of the application.

bashCopy code

```
# Example command to run unit tests ./gradlew test
```

bashCopy code

```
# Example command to run integration tests ./gradlew integrationTest
```

Automated tests are essential for detecting bugs, regressions, and performance issues early in the development process. By automating testing, developers can ensure that changes to the codebase do not introduce unintended side effects and maintain the overall quality of the application.

Once the application has been successfully built and tested, the final stage of the CI/CD pipeline involves deploying the application to a target environment, such as a staging or production server.

bashCopy code

Example command to deploy the application to a staging environment ansible-playbook deploy-staging.yml
bashCopy code
Example command to deploy the application to a production environment ansible-playbook deploy-production.yml
Automating the deployment process eliminates manual intervention, reduces the risk of human error, and enables rapid and consistent releases. Additionally, deploying the application to staging environments allows for further testing and validation before releasing to production, ensuring a smooth and error-free deployment process.
In addition to CI/CD pipelines, other automation techniques can be employed to streamline the app deployment and testing processes. For example, infrastructure as code (IaC) tools like Terraform or CloudFormation can be used to automate the provisioning and configuration of infrastructure resources, such as servers, databases, and networking components.
bashCopy code
Example command to provision infrastructure resources using Terraform terraform apply
By defining infrastructure resources as code, developers can easily replicate and scale environments, ensure consistency across different environments, and reduce the time and effort required to manage infrastructure manually.
Furthermore, automated monitoring and alerting systems can be integrated into the deployment process to detect and respond to issues in real-time. Tools like Prometheus and Grafana can be used to monitor application performance, track key metrics, and generate alerts when anomalies or failures occur.
bashCopy code

Example command to deploy monitoring and alerting stack using Prometheus and Grafana helm install prometheus stable/prometheus helm install grafana stable/grafana

Automating monitoring and alerting allows development teams to proactively identify and address issues before they impact end-users, ensuring the reliability and availability of the application.

In summary, automating app deployment and testing processes is essential for accelerating the software development lifecycle, improving the quality and reliability of applications, and enabling teams to deliver value to end-users more quickly and efficiently. By leveraging CI/CD pipelines, infrastructure as code, and automated monitoring and alerting, organizations can achieve greater agility, scalability, and resilience in their software delivery practices.

Chapter 9: Exploring Advanced Architectural Patterns and Design Principles

Understanding advanced architectural patterns like Model-View-Presenter (MVP), Model-View-ViewModel (MVVM), and Clean Architecture is crucial for building scalable, maintainable, and testable Android applications. These architectural patterns provide guidelines and best practices for structuring code and separating concerns, resulting in codebases that are easier to understand, extend, and maintain over time.

MVP, MVVM, and Clean Architecture are variations of the traditional Model-View-Controller (MVC) pattern, each with its own strengths and trade-offs. In MVP, the responsibilities of the MVC pattern are divided into three main components: Model, View, and Presenter. The Model represents the data and business logic of the application, the View is responsible for rendering the user interface and handling user input, and the Presenter acts as an intermediary between the Model and View, handling business logic and updating the View based on changes in the Model.

javaCopy code

```
// Example of MVP architecture in Android public interface MainContract { interface View { void showData(String data); } interface Presenter { void fetchData(); } }
```

javaCopy code

```
public class MainPresenter implements MainContract.Presenter { private MainContract.View view; public MainPresenter(MainContract.View view) { this.view = view; } @Override public void fetchData() { // Retrieve
```

data from Model String data = getDataFromModel(); // Update View with data view.showData(data); } }

javaCopy code

```
public class MainActivity extends AppCompatActivity implements MainContract.View { private MainContract.Presenter presenter; @Override protected void onCreate(Bundle savedInstanceState) { super.onCreate(savedInstanceState); setContentView(R.layout.activity_main); presenter = new MainPresenter(this); presenter.fetchData(); } @Override public void showData(String data) { // Display data in UI } }
```

MVVM, on the other hand, introduces a new component called ViewModel, which is responsible for managing the presentation logic and state of the View. In MVVM, the View observes changes in the ViewModel and updates itself accordingly, while the ViewModel interacts with the Model to retrieve and manipulate data.

javaCopy code

```
// Example of MVVM architecture in Android public class MainViewModel extends ViewModel { private MutableLiveData<String> data; public MainViewModel() { data = new MutableLiveData<>(); fetchData(); } public LiveData<String> getData() { return data; } private void fetchData() { // Retrieve data from Model String newData = getDataFromModel(); // Update data LiveData data.setValue(newData); } }
```

javaCopy code

```
public class MainActivity extends AppCompatActivity { @Override protected void onCreate(Bundle savedInstanceState) { super.onCreate(savedInstanceState);
```

setContentView(R.layout.activity_main); MainViewModel viewModel = new ViewModelProvider(this).get(MainViewModel.class); viewModel.getData().observe(this, newData -> { // Update UI with new data }); } }

Clean Architecture, proposed by Robert C. Martin, emphasizes the separation of concerns and the independence of application layers. In Clean Architecture, the application is divided into multiple layers, each with its own set of responsibilities and dependencies. The inner layers contain business logic and domain-specific code, while the outer layers deal with framework-specific concerns such as user interface and data persistence.

javaCopy code

```
// Example of Clean Architecture layers in Android public interface Repository { String fetchData(); } public class DataRepository implements Repository { @Override public String fetchData() { // Retrieve data from data source return "Data from repository"; } }
```

javaCopy code

```
public class UseCase { private Repository repository; public UseCase(Repository repository) { this.repository = repository; } public String fetchData() { return repository.fetchData(); } }
```

javaCopy code

```
public class MainActivity extends AppCompatActivity { @Override protected void onCreate(Bundle savedInstanceState) { super.onCreate(savedInstanceState); setContentView(R.layout.activity_main); Repository repository = new DataRepository(); UseCase useCase =
```

new UseCase(repository); String data = useCase.fetchData(); // Update UI with data } }

Overall, understanding advanced architectural patterns like MVP, MVVM, and Clean Architecture is essential for building scalable, maintainable, and testable Android applications. These patterns provide clear guidelines for organizing code and separating concerns, enabling developers to create robust and flexible software that can easily adapt to changing requirements and business needs.

Applying SOLID principles for robust and maintainable code is essential for developing high-quality software that is easy to understand, extend, and maintain over time. SOLID is an acronym that stands for five key principles of object-oriented design: Single Responsibility Principle (SRP), Open/Closed Principle (OCP), Liskov Substitution Principle (LSP), Interface Segregation Principle (ISP), and Dependency Inversion Principle (DIP). By adhering to these principles, developers can create codebases that are more flexible, modular, and resilient to changes.

The Single Responsibility Principle (SRP) states that a class should have only one reason to change, meaning that each class should have a single responsibility or purpose. This principle encourages developers to break down complex systems into smaller, more manageable components, each responsible for a specific task or functionality.

javaCopy code

// Example of Single Responsibility Principle public class UserManager { private UserRepository userRepository; public UserManager(UserRepository userRepository) { this.userRepository = userRepository; } public void createUser(User user) { // Validate user input // Persist user data to database userRepository.save(user); } public

User getUserById(int userId) { // Retrieve user data from database return userRepository.findById(userId); } }

The Open/Closed Principle (OCP) states that software entities (classes, modules, functions, etc.) should be open for extension but closed for modification. This means that existing code should not be modified to accommodate new requirements or features. Instead, new functionality should be added through extension or composition, without altering existing code.

javaCopy code

```
// Example of Open/Closed Principle public interface Shape { double calculateArea(); } public class Circle implements Shape { private double radius; public Circle(double radius) { this.radius = radius; } @Override public double calculateArea() { return Math.PI * radius * radius; } } public class Rectangle implements Shape { private double width; private double height; public Rectangle(double width, double height) { this.width = width; this.height = height; } @Override public double calculateArea() { return width * height; } }
```

The Liskov Substitution Principle (LSP) states that objects of a superclass should be replaceable with objects of its subclass without affecting the correctness of the program. This principle ensures that subclasses adhere to the contracts established by their superclass and maintain the same behavior and semantics.

javaCopy code

```
// Example of Liskov Substitution Principle public class Rectangle { protected int width; protected int height; public void setWidth(int width) { this.width = width; } public void setHeight(int height) { this.height = height; }
```

public int calculateArea() { return width * height; } } public class Square extends Rectangle { @Override public void setWidth(int width) { super.setWidth(width); super.setHeight(width); } @Override public void setHeight(int height) { super.setWidth(height); super.setHeight(height); } }

The Interface Segregation Principle (ISP) states that clients should not be forced to depend on interfaces they do not use. This principle encourages developers to design fine-grained interfaces that are specific to the needs of the clients that use them, rather than creating large, monolithic interfaces that cater to multiple clients.

javaCopy code

// Example of Interface Segregation Principle public interface Document { void print(); void fax(); void scan(); } public class Printer implements Document { @Override public void print() { // Implementation } @Override public void fax() { throw new UnsupportedOperationException("Not supported"); } @Override public void scan() { throw new UnsupportedOperationException("Not supported"); } } public class Scanner implements Document { @Override public void print() { throw new UnsupportedOperationException("Not supported"); } @Override public void fax() { throw new UnsupportedOperationException("Not supported"); } @Override public void scan() { // Implementation } }

The Dependency Inversion Principle (DIP) states that high-level modules should not depend on low-level modules. Instead, both should depend on abstractions. This principle promotes loose coupling between classes and modules by relying on interfaces or abstract classes to define dependencies, rather than concrete implementations.

javaCopy code

```
// Example of Dependency Inversion Principle public interface NotificationService { void sendNotification(String message); } public class EmailNotificationService implements NotificationService { @Override public void sendNotification(String message) { // Implementation } } public class SMSNotificationService implements NotificationService { @Override public void sendNotification(String message) { // Implementation } } public class NotificationManager { private NotificationService notificationService; public NotificationManager(NotificationService notificationService) { this.notificationService = notificationService; } public void sendNotification(String message) { notificationService.sendNotification(message); } }
```

By applying SOLID principles, developers can create codebases that are more modular, flexible, and maintainable, resulting in software that is easier to understand, extend, and debug. These principles provide guidelines for writing clean, robust, and scalable code that can adapt to changing requirements and evolve over time.

Chapter 10: Beyond Android Studio: Integrating with Other Development Tools and Technologies

Integrating Android Studio with other development tools like Docker and Kubernetes can significantly enhance the development workflow and streamline the deployment process. Docker is a containerization platform that allows developers to package applications and their dependencies into portable containers, while Kubernetes is an open-source container orchestration platform for automating deployment, scaling, and management of containerized applications. By integrating Android Studio with Docker and Kubernetes, developers can build, test, and deploy Android applications more efficiently across different environments.

One of the primary benefits of integrating Android Studio with Docker is the ability to create consistent development environments across different machines and operating systems. Docker containers encapsulate all the dependencies required for running an application, including the operating system, libraries, and runtime environment, ensuring that the application behaves the same way regardless of the underlying infrastructure. This eliminates the "it works on my machine" problem and makes it easier for developers to collaborate on projects.

To integrate Android Studio with Docker, developers can use the Android Emulator to run Android applications inside Docker containers. This allows developers to test their applications in isolated environments that closely resemble production settings, ensuring compatibility and reliability. The Android Emulator provides a convenient way to create and manage virtual devices for testing different Android versions and configurations, making it easier to identify and fix compatibility issues.

bashCopy code

```
# Command to run Android Emulator inside a Docker container docker run -d --privileged -v /dev/kvm:/dev/kvm -p 5555:5555 -p 5554:5554 -p 5900:5900 androidstudio/android-emulator
```

Additionally, integrating Android Studio with Kubernetes enables developers to deploy and manage Android applications in a scalable and resilient manner. Kubernetes provides powerful features for orchestrating containerized workloads, such as automatic scaling, rolling updates, and service discovery, which can help streamline the deployment process and improve application reliability.

To deploy an Android application to Kubernetes, developers can use tools like Skaffold, which automates the build, push, and deployment process for Kubernetes applications. Skaffold integrates seamlessly with Android Studio, allowing developers to deploy their applications to a Kubernetes cluster with a single command.

bashCopy code

```
# Command to deploy Android application to Kubernetes using Skaffold skaffold run
```

By integrating Android Studio with Docker and Kubernetes, developers can take advantage of modern development practices such as containerization and orchestration to build, test, and deploy Android applications more efficiently. This enables faster iteration cycles, smoother collaboration between teams, and improved overall productivity. Additionally, by leveraging the scalability and resilience of Kubernetes, developers can ensure that their applications can handle increasing workloads and remain available under high demand.

In summary, integrating Android Studio with Docker and Kubernetes offers numerous benefits for Android developers, including consistent development environments, streamlined deployment processes, and improved application reliability. By adopting these tools and practices, developers can accelerate the development lifecycle, reduce time-to-market, and deliver high-quality Android applications that meet the demands of today's users.

Exploring cross-platform development frameworks like Flutter and React Native opens up a world of possibilities for developers seeking to build mobile applications that run seamlessly across multiple platforms. These frameworks offer an alternative to traditional platform-specific development, allowing developers to write code once and deploy it on both iOS and Android devices. Flutter, developed by Google, and React Native, maintained by Facebook, are two of the most popular cross-platform frameworks available today, each with its own set of features, advantages, and use cases.

Flutter, built on the Dart programming language, is known for its fast performance, expressive UI components, and hot reload feature, which enables developers to see changes to their code in real-time without restarting the application. Flutter provides a rich set of pre-designed widgets and layout options, making it easy to create beautiful and responsive user interfaces that look and feel native on both iOS and Android devices.

bashCopy code

```
# Command to create a new Flutter project flutter create my_flutter_app
```

Flutter's architecture, based on the concept of widgets, allows developers to compose complex UIs using a hierarchical structure of reusable components. This enables rapid development and easy maintenance of applications, as developers can easily refactor and rearrange widgets to accommodate changes in requirements or design.

dartCopy code

```
// Example of a Flutter widget import 'package:flutter/material.dart'; class MyApp extends StatelessWidget { @override Widget build(BuildContext context) { return MaterialApp( title: 'My App', home: Scaffold( appBar: AppBar( title: Text('Welcome to Flutter'), ), body: Center( child: Text('Hello, World!'), ), ), ); } }
```

React Native, on the other hand, leverages JavaScript and the React framework to build cross-platform mobile applications. React Native allows developers to write code in JavaScript and JSX, a syntax extension that enables the use of XML-like tags to describe the structure of UI components. React Native applications are built using a combination of JavaScript and native UI components, resulting in high performance and a native look and feel.

bashCopy code

```
# Command to create a new React Native project npx react-native init MyReactNativeApp
```

One of the key advantages of React Native is its large and active community, which provides a wealth of third-party libraries, tools, and resources to help developers build and maintain their applications. Additionally, React Native's "learn once, write anywhere" philosophy allows developers familiar with web development to quickly transition to mobile development, as many concepts and patterns from React.js can be applied to React Native development.

javascriptCopy code

```
// Example of a React Native component import React from 'react'; import { View, Text } from 'react-native'; const App = () => { return ( <View style={{ flex: 1, justifyContent: 'center', alignItems: 'center' }}> <Text>Welcome to React Native</Text> </View> ); }; export default App;
```

While both Flutter and React Native offer powerful tools and capabilities for cross-platform development, they each have their own strengths and weaknesses that may influence the choice of framework for a particular project. Flutter's strong focus on performance, hot reload feature, and rich set of UI components make it an excellent choice for building highly interactive and visually appealing applications. On the other hand, React Native's familiarity to web developers, extensive community support, and seamless integration with existing JavaScript libraries and frameworks make it a compelling option for projects with existing web assets or a large JavaScript codebase.

In summary, exploring cross-platform development frameworks like Flutter and React Native provides developers with the flexibility and versatility to create mobile applications that can reach a broader audience across different platforms. By leveraging these frameworks, developers can streamline the development process, reduce time-to-market, and deliver high-quality applications that meet the needs and expectations of today's users. Whether choosing Flutter or React Native depends on various factors such as project requirements, team expertise, and long-term goals, both frameworks offer powerful solutions for building modern mobile applications.

Conclusion

In this comprehensive book bundle, "Android Studio Masterclass: Android IDE for App Developers," we have covered a wide range of topics aimed at empowering both novice and experienced developers to harness the full potential of Android Studio. From the fundamental principles of app development explored in "Android Studio Essentials: A Beginner's Guide" to the advanced techniques and optimizations detailed in "Advanced Android Development Techniques: Mastering Android Studio" and "Optimizing Performance in Android Studio: Expert Strategies for Efficient App Development," this bundle offers a holistic approach to mastering the Android development environment.

Through the exploration of various tools, techniques, and best practices presented in each book, readers have gained valuable insights into the intricacies of Android app development, from building basic applications to optimizing performance and efficiency. Additionally, "Android Studio Pro: Advanced Tools and Tips for Power Users" delves into advanced features and customization options within Android Studio, equipping developers with the knowledge and skills needed to elevate their development workflow and productivity.

As the Android ecosystem continues to evolve and expand, the knowledge acquired from this masterclass bundle will serve as a solid foundation for developers to stay ahead of the curve and create innovative and impactful applications. Whether you are just starting your journey in Android development or seeking to refine your skills and expertise, the insights and techniques shared in this bundle will undoubtedly propel your development journey to new heights. With a combination of practical guidance, expert strategies, and advanced tools, "Android Studio Masterclass" is your definitive resource for becoming a proficient and successful Android app developer.

www.ingramcontent.com/pod-product-compliance
Lightning Source LLC
Chambersburg PA
CBHW071233050326
40690CB00011B/2097